JOY OF LIVING BIBLE STUDY SERIES

DISCOVERING GOD'S POWER

Studies in Genesis 1—17

Life-related for Personal and Group Study

DORIS W. GREIG

Regal Books

A Division of GL Publications
Ventura, California, U.S.A.

Published by Regal Books
A Division of GL Publications
Ventura, California 93006
Printed in U.S.A.

Scripture quotations used in this publication are taken from:

KJV—King James Version.
NASB—New American Standard Bible. © The Lockman Foundation 1960, 1962, 1963, 1968, 1971, 1972, 1973, 1975. Used by permission.
NIV—Scripture quotations marked *(NIV)* are from the HOLY BIBLE: NEW INTERNATIONAL VERSION. Copyright © 1973, 1978, 1984 International Bible Society. Used by permission of Zondervan Bible Publishers.
NKJV—New King James Version, Holy Bible. Copyright © 1979, 1980, 1982 by Thomas Nelson Inc., Publishers. Used by permission.
TEV—Good News Bible, The Bible in Today's English Version. Old Testament copyright © American Bible Society 1966. New Testament copyright © American Bible Society 1966, 1971, 1976. Used by permission.
TLB—The Living Bible, Copyright © 1971 by Tyndale House Publishers, Wheaton, Illinois. Used by permission.

Any omission of credits or permissions granted is unintentional. The publisher requests documentation for future printings.

Library of Congress Cataloging-in-Publication Data

Greig, Doris W., 1926-
    Discovering God's power.

    1. Bible. O.T. Genesis I-XVII—Study.
I. Title.
BS1235.5.G74   1989   222'.1106   88-32494
ISBN 0-8307-1344-1

1 2 3 4 5 6 7 8 9 10 / 91 90 89

Rights for publishing this book in other languages are contracted by Gospel Literature International (GLINT) foundation. GLINT also provides technical help for the adaptation, translation, and publishing of Bible study resources and books in scores of languages worldwide. For further information, contact GLINT, Post Office Box 488, Rosemead, California, 91770, U.S.A., or the publisher.

CONTENTS

HOW TO GET THE MOST FROM THIS BOOK

The Bible is a living book! It is relevant and powerful, but more than that, it is the active voice of our living God, and He wants to communicate with you daily through His Word. As you study the Bible, you will learn about God's person and character. You will begin to find His purpose for your life as He speaks to you through His written Word. His purpose is unchanging and His principles are unfailing guidelines for living. He will show us His truth and what our response should be to it.

Will you set aside a special time each day to interact with God in His Word? As you read, study, meditate and memorize His Word, the Holy Spirit will guide you, and His direction for your life will be made clear. More and more, His voice will be easily discerned in the din of life's pressures. When your heart is available and you see God's good intentions for you, you will then learn how to respond to the Lord's personal call to you day by day, moment by moment. As you train your ears to hear the voice of God, you will recognize His presence in the most unlikely circumstances and places. "The grass withers and the flowers fail, but the word of our God stands forever" (Isaiah 40:8, NIV).

Try to have several versions of the Bible available as you study. Comparing these versions will enrich your understanding of a passage and bring added insight. Try not to use a commentary or any other reference work until you have allowed the Lord to speak personally to you through His Word.

Each lesson begins with a section of *Study Notes*. After Lesson 1, the introductory lesson, these Notes suggest ways to understand the passage at hand and relate it to other biblical teaching. Following the *Study Notes* is a section of *Questions,* designed to guide your Bible study through a six-day week. On the first day the previous Notes are

5

reviewed. And Days 2-6 will prepare you for the next lesson. You will benefit most from your study if you will do each day's questions at a regular time.

This study is designed to be used individually or in a group. If you are studying in a group, we urge you to actively share your answers and thoughts. In sharing we give encouragement to others and learn from one another.

This book has been conveniently hole-punched and perforated for easy tearout and insertion in a 6″ × 9½″ looseleaf notebook:

- Bible study pages lie flat in your notebook for ease of writing as you study.

- Additional notebook paper can be inserted for journaling or more extensive notes and other relevant information.

- Additional studies in the Joy of Living Series can be inserted, along with your personal notes, and tabbed to help you build your Bible study file for easy, future reference.

May God bless you as you begin your journey into His Word. This may be the first time for you to take this trip, or it may be that you have journeyed this way many times before. No matter what trip it is for you, we pray you will find new joy and hope as you seek to live in the light of the living God!

INTRODUCTION TO GENESIS

Study Notes

Genesis portrays Jesus Christ, our Creator, God. The word "genesis" came into the English language by way of Latin from the Greek. Genesis means "origin, or source, or beginning." This name was given to the first book of the Bible when it was translated into the Greek in the third century B.C.

All Our Beginnings Are in God

Genesis is the book of beginnings. *It gives the account of the beginning of all that the Creator brought into being.* Genesis answers our questions concerning the origin of the world, and of plant, animal and human life.

Genesis also records the beginning of a particular race of people, the Jewish people, who would safeguard this revelation by recording the holy Word of God as the Spirit of God led them. "For no prophecy recorded in Scripture was ever thought up by the prophet himself. It was the Holy Spirit within these godly men who gave them true messages from God" (2 Peter 1:20-21).

Genesis could be called the book of beginnings, for it records for us the beginning of the world, man, sin, civilization, nations, agriculture, machinery, music and poetry. It tells us of the world's first marriage, the first child born, the first murder committed, the first drunkenness, the first kingdom established and the first heathen temple. But the most wonderful thing that Genesis records for us is the beginning of God's work toward man and the promise of His Son, the Lord Jesus Christ, to us. Genesis reveals God's plans and purposes in His dealings with men.

7

We Meet the Divine
and Human Authors of Genesis

The author of the original book of Genesis is not known. It is safe to say that Moses by inspiration of the Holy Spirit is the final coordinating author of the book. However, the main part of Genesis occurred before Moses' life on earth, and therefore may originally have been written in different sections or repeated verbally from generation to generation until the time of Moses. Moses, by the inspiration of the Holy Spirit, put together into one book the story of Genesis for us, as God led him to write. Moses was prepared to understand the records, manuscripts and oral narratives by his training in "wisdom of the Egyptians" (Acts 7:22). He was a prophet who was granted the great privilege of unhurried hours of communion with God on Sinai (Exodus 19:3; 24:18; 34:2).

Obviously the men who first recorded the story of Creation fully believed that they were indeed recording the truth of God's creating power. The Bible tells us that God talked with Adam and Eve in the Garden of Eden (Genesis 2:16,17). God possibly told them the story of the Creation of the universe in a way that they could easily understand while they were in the Garden of Eden.

Some Bible scholars suggest that the unknown past of the Creation was revealed to the original writer of these chapters by a vision, just as John the Apostle wrote the last book of the Bible, Revelation, by a vision that was revealed to him (Revelation 1:19). Since there were no eye witnesses to God's creation, the first chapters of Genesis are a direct communication of God to someone. We need not be disturbed by the conflict of so-called scientific discoveries, but rather we are content to realize that eventually even science will have to come into agreement with the Word of God, which is forever settled in the heavens.

Let us never forget the importance of the phrase "In the beginning God created" (Genesis 1:1). *Around the Word of God is the protection of the Holy Spirit of God who inspired its words.*

Who wrote or told the Creation story used by Moses? Possibly it was written long before by Abraham, Noah or Enoch. Who knows? Writing was in common use before the day of Abraham. In Ur, as in every important city in Babylonia, there were libraries with thousands of books, dictionaries, grammars, reference works, encyclopedias, works on mathematics, astrology, geography, religion and politics.

Possibly Abraham had received traditions or records from Shem about the story of Creation, of the fall of man and of the flood. Abraham lived in a society of culture, books, and libraries. He probably

8

made careful and accurate copies of all that happened to him and of the promises that God had made to him. He put it down on clay tablets in the cuneiform writing to be handed down in the annals of the nation he was founding.

Thus Genesis records for us the beginning of everything except God. Without Genesis our knowledge of a creating God would be pitifully limited; we would be ignorant of the beginnings of our universe.

We Find Jesus in Genesis

Jesus Christ is the center of the Bible. He is somewhere on every page. In Genesis we see Him in type and prophecy in:
1. seed of the woman—Genesis 3:15
2. skins of slain beasts—Genesis 3:21
3. Abel's blood sacrifice necessary—Genesis 4:4
4. entrance into the ark of safety—Genesis 7:1,7
5. offering up of Isaac—Genesis 22
6. Joseph lifted from the pit to the throne—Genesis 37:28; 41:41-44

Genesis Is Beyond Science

Although the Bible is not intended to be a textbook of science, its words are completely true. The Genesis account is not a scientific account, yet it is accurate in every detail and can be completely trusted. *Genesis does not attempt to grapple with or answer technical scientific questions. It deals with matters far beyond the realm of science.*

Scientist Dr. George F. Howe, who holds that creationism is no less "scientific" than the general theory of evolution, believes the Genesis record of beginnings is beyond the understanding of science because scientists cannot explain or repeat miracles. God works by miracles, says Dr. Howe, in contrast to scientists who work by method and measurement. Obviously, scientists cannot study or repeat Creation in the laboratory, so they attempt to explain it by a theory.

Any Christian accepting in faith the miracles in Christ's life has no difficulty in accepting also that when God chose to create, He spoke and that which He spoke took shape. In other words, says Howe, God said it and it was so. And Howe reminds us that God is not going to stage a daily creation miracle just to satisfy man's curiosity, no more than does a contractor leave a bulldozer outside a building he has erected simply to prove that he used bulldozers in its construction.

The Bible seeks to reveal the sacred meaning of God's being and purpose and His dealing with His creatures as He works out His plan for this world. A man of faith will accept Hebrews 11:3 at face value; "By faith—by believing God—we know that the world and the stars—in fact, all things—were made at God's command; and that they were all made from things that can't be seen." Thus we are content to realize that eventually science will come to an agreement with the Word of God, which is forever settled in the heavens.

God Acts in Creation and Redemption

The key to what Genesis teaches is found, therefore, in the sublime statement, "In the beginning God." God came down first to create and then to save. Compare the work of God in creation and His work in redemption. He merely spoke and worlds were formed; but in Christ He had to suffer and die to save His creation. He made man by His breath; He saved man by His death (John 3:16).

Many scholars think that the Bible is inharmonious and full of errors. That perspective is similar to taking a phonograph record and boring a hole a little off center and putting it on a machine to play. What a disharmony results! The sound is indescribable. Such people take the Bible from its inspired setting and have it revolve around their own speculations and ideas.

Yet the Bible says: "In the beginning God." It does not say, "In the beginning man." The "book of beginnings" begins with God— creation begins with God. There is a tremendous sweep in these first few verses of Genesis. Everything points back to God, and yet how prone we are to forget Him! We do not count Him in the beginning of all things, even in our lives.

Our eyes are fixed on circumstances and things about us instead of on God. So many people live just within the little circle of their own experiences. It would do us all good if we would read Genesis 1:1 and stop after the word, "God." *Yes, in the very beginning of creation, in the beginning of the very first day, God was there. Is He in the beginning of every one of your days?* What a difference it would make in your life if He were! This study will help you have Him in the beginning of every one of your days. If you will follow the daily plan and begin your day with prayer and then read the Bible using the questions which are prepared for each day, what a difference you will see in your life!

We See God with Spiritual Sight

God is the beginning of all, and He is everywhere. Though we cannot see God, except by our spiritual sight, we can see evidences

10

of Him in all His creation. As Paul declared in Romans 1:20, "Since the creation of the world His invisible attributes are clearly seen, being understood by the things that are made, even His eternal power and Godhead."

No one finds anything in this universe that God has not put there first for man to find. A party had climbed to the top of the Matterhorn. They were admiring the grandeur and beauty all about them. One of the climbers had a microscope to study insect life. He looked through the microscope at the legs of a little fly. "See," he said, "the legs of the house fly in America are naked, but the legs of this little creature are covered with fur leggings. The same God who made this great mountain has attended to the comfort of His tiniest of creatures, even supplying it with socks and mitts."

Truly, God's hand is in evidence in all His creation. "The heavens declare the glory of God; and the firmament sheweth forth his handywork" (Psalm 19:1).

Faith Is Important to Believer and Scientist

Evolutionary process demands a first cause, a beginning, but it cannot supply it. Evolutionists must tell us where the universe came from. In discussing the many problems presented by evolutionary theory, Dr. George Howe points out that evolutionists have to explain more than just how that first bit of matter was formed. Their greatest problem is one of first cause, one of beginning. Who or what caused matter to come into existence?

Evolutionists and philosophers admit, naturally enough, the eternity of elementary matter, from which, they state, through a slow evolution, everything has been produced—heaven, earth, man, and even God, if He is necessary. Science deals only with phenomena, or with the things that are perceived by the senses. That is, things we can see, feel, taste, smell, or hear.

Can God be seen by the human eye or by the most powerful microscope? Can He be caught in a test tube or weighed in the most delicate balance? "Canst thou by searching find out God?" (Job 11:7).

Science starts with some tremendous assumptions about the laws and order of the universe, and these assumptions are on pure faith. They never have been and never can be proved by scientific study. Yet the scientist never doubts them. He also keeps on using faith through much of his work. When an astronomer locates three points on the orbit of a planet, he constructs the whole orbit and looks for the planet at other points, and confidently expects to find it there. With faith and imagination he predicts and looks for the unseen. The

11

astronomer, by faith, predicts an eclipse of the sun; he tells you the very day, hour, and minute it will begin.

This is only one of a thousand instances of facts that are predicted on faith. Men cannot predict history in the future and they cannot foretell when a war will break out, because history is made by man. But astronomers, for instance, can predict just what will take place in nature, because the heavens are timed by God whose timepiece is perfect. Astronomers used to tell of things that frighten us; now they see things that frighten them!

We know that light travels at a rate of 186,000 miles per second. At this tremendous rate of speed, light takes about one and one-fourth seconds to reach the earth from the moon, and about eight minutes from the sun. From the nearest star, light travels four years on its journey to the earth. But to get here from the nearest Spiro Galaxy (one great system of stars like our Milky Way), light must travel two million years. And from the farthest galaxy that can be photographed with the two hundred inch telescope on Mt. Palomar, light travels for over one billion years before it reaches the earth.

Josephus, the great Jewish historian, said that "God adorned the heavens with the sun, moon, and stars." How little did he realize that the Milky Way alone is composed of billions of stars and it would take a hundred thousand years to go from its one edge to the other traveling at the speed of light. Our earth and its solar system are only a speck in this vast ocean of stars. The Bible says in Genesis 1:31, "God saw everything that he had made, and, behold, it was very good."

True Science Harmonizes with the Bible

The question is often asked: "Does science contradict the Bible?" True science and the Bible illuminate each other. Dr. Michael Pupin, a renowned physicist and a Christian, firmly believed that unless science assisted him in achieving a better understanding of Creation, in gaining a more personal relationship with the Lord, and in carrying out God's divine purpose, then he had failed as a scientist.

If true believers knew science, and scientists knew the Bible, there would be more Christian faith, and more true philosophy. The laws of God's Word spurn the ever-changing theories of men. Galileo numbered the stars in thousands. Did God ever make a mistake like that? Long before that, God had told Abraham to look up into the heavens. He promised Abraham seed as innumerable as the stars (Genesis 15:5).

The early scientists thought the world was flat, that it rested on the back of a turtle. What does God's Word say? "He . . . hangeth the

12

earth upon nothing" (Job 26:7), and God "sitteth upon the circle of the earth" (Isaiah 40:22).

Now that scientists have discovered that the stars are literally without number, their terminology fits in with the Scriptures. Since men have gone out into space, many of them have attested to the fact that it is only God who could have created the order that they have seen in space. Eugene A. Cernan, one of America's astronauts, has stated his conviction that the universe "didn't happen by accident." Commenting on his view of earth from a quarter-million miles away, he marveled at the planet's size, beauty and perfection. He noted there were no strings to hold it up, no fulcrum that it rested upon. He was awed by the infinity of space and time, as he came to appreciate them while in orbit. Enjoying his privileged perspective of earth, he said it made him feel selfish, seeing earth perhaps as God does now and as He did when He created it. Cernan came out of his experience convinced of God's existence because of the order he observed while in space.

Yes, surely, we look at the universe and say, "Oh, Lord, how great Thou art."

Study Questions

Before you begin your study this week:
1. Pray and ask God to speak to you through His Holy Spirit each day.
2. Use only your Bible for your answers.
3. Write your answers and the verses you have used.
4. Challenge questions are for those who have the time and wish to do them.
5. Personal questions are to be shared with your study group only if you wish to share.
6. As you study look for a verse to memorize this week. Write it down, carry it with you, tack it to your bulletin board, tape it to the dashboard of your car. Make a real effort to learn the verse and its reference.

FIRST DAY: Read all of the preceding notes and look up all of the Scriptures.

1. What was a helpful or new thought from the introduction to Genesis?

2. What was the most meaningful Scripture from the notes to you personally?

3. (Personal) Have you chosen to take up the challenge to give daily time to this study and to God? What sacrifice has God shown you that you could make to give time to Him in study and prayer? (Share if possible with your group, as it may help someone else.)

SECOND DAY: Read all of Genesis 1, concentrating on Genesis 1:1-8.

1. List the verses where you find the phrases "God created" or "God said" and record with the verse what you learn God created by His Word.

2. God spoke and by His Word created. Read and record what the following verses say about God, the Creator of all things.

   Colossians 1:16

   Psalm 8:3-5

   Psalm 33:6

   Hebrews 11:3

3. What did God see after He created each thing? What did God see in Genesis 1:31 when He surveyed everything that He had made?

4 a. What does Psalm 121:2 tell you about God, the Creator?

   b. (Personal) Apply this thought to your own life.

5. What is our attitude to be if we have God as our help? Read Psalm 146:5,6.

15

6 a. Read John 1:1-4. The "Word" is Jesus Christ. What do you learn about Him in these verses?

   b. Compare John 14:6 with John 1:4. What does each one say about life?

   c. What is the only way to God the Father according to John 14:6?

   d. (Personal) Have you ever come to God by the only way, as given in John 14:6?

THIRD DAY: Read Genesis 1:9-19.

1. Describe what God said about water and dry land on the third day of Creation.

2. Describe the vegetation God created on the third day.

3. Challenge: Find the word *God* in all of *chapter 1* and list the words found after His name which help us to know what He is like. Circle each *new* word as you find it. Example: 1 God—created.

4. As you have discovered these words describing God and what He did in Creation, which one meant the most to you because it helped you to sense His love for you as an individual?

5 a. What did God create on the fourth day?

b. What was the purpose of this creation?

6. What three things do you learn about God from Jeremiah 10:12?

FOURTH DAY: Read Genesis 1:20-25.

1. Describe what God created on the fifth day. Be specific.

2. Challenge: What do you think the phrase "according to its kind" means (Genesis 1:21)? Connect this phrase to the words "be fruitful and multiply" in Genesis 1:22.

3. What did God create on the sixth day according to Genesis 1?

4. What does Isaiah 45:18 say was the reason God created the earth?

5. Read Psalm 8. Choose your favorite verse and share why you chose it.

6. Psalm 8:6-8 speaks of man's responsibility on earth. Considering ecological needs of today, how do you think the Christian should conduct himself in this area?

FIFTH DAY: Read Genesis 1:26-31.

1. What was man created to be like?

2. **Challenge:** What significance do you find in the word "our" in Genesis 1:26? Could this relate to the Trinity?

3. What do the following verses say to you about the Trinity? Put these verses into your own words.

   Titus 3:4-6

   Hebrews 9:14

   1 Peter 1:2

4. Record what God did and said in Genesis 1:28.

5. How does Acts 17:26 relate to these words of God in Genesis 1:28?

6. What do you find in Jeremiah 32:17 which encourages you today?

SIXTH DAY: Read Psalm 104, a Psalm of creation.

1. Find verses that illustrate the power of God's creation.

2. Find verses that illustrate the beauty of God's creation.

3. Find verses that portray God as our loving Father who cares for each of us.

4. Find verses that illustrate how wonderfully God provided for the animals and birds on earth.

5. Choose some verses of praise to God that the psalmist recorded, and put them into your own words.

6 a. Psalm 104:31-34 could be used for a prayer. Put this into your own words. Could this be a part of your prayer today as you think of God's wonderful creation?

   b. What verse did you choose to memorize this week? Why did you choose it?

19

GOD'S CREATION: OUR BEGINNINGS
GENESIS 1

Study Notes

How can you know that God created the universe when you weren't there at the time and do not understand how He did it?

If you look closely, you will find the name of the One who was both architect and builder of this universe. Where do you first see it? In the first verse of the Bible!

An automobile, a pen, a washing machine—almost anything manufactured—bears the name of its maker on it. Just so, nature itself—in the rocks, the flowers, the birds—bears His name, giving evidence of God as a great architect.

Look at the stars. The skies are filled with stars that only God could have made. "The heavens are telling of the glory of God; their expanse is declaring the work of His hands" (Psalm 19:1).

Our Universe Didn't Just Happen

Some try to tell us that this marvelous universe was brought into being by chance. But that is hardly a sufficient explanation. Though we cannot fully understand how God made this universe, it isn't reasonable to think that mere forces made such an intricately, beautifully, carefully planned world without a great mind to direct those forces.

According to Genesis 1:3, God just spoke, and it was done. God used the great forces of the universe to bring about His marvelous creation. In other words, Creation of the universe took the mind of God plus the elements. No explanation or answer that leaves out God is sufficient.

A mechanic may have all the parts of an automobile lying at his feet, but it will take his master mind to make an automobile out of them. Just so, the jet engine, the helicopter and the skyscraper are products of the mind, not chance. And this universe is infinitely greater and more complex than the greatest manufactured product devised by human intelligence.

You can solve any problem in mathematics with just 10 digits or numbers. But you do not try to solve a problem by putting a lot of numbers in a hat and shaking them around. It takes the 10 numbers *plus* your mind to work out the correct answer.

If a poet wants to write a beautiful poem, he does not put a lot of letters from the alphabet into a hat and shake out a poem. Rather, he tells us his thoughts by arranging those letters in his mind to create the beautiful result we call poetry.

In a factory, it takes a girl two days to learn how to put together the 17 parts of a meat chopper. You could shake these 17 parts together in a tub for the next 17 million years, but you would never have a meat chopper.

Similarly, we know it would be impossible for the more than 90 elements comprising this universe to combine by mere chance into this wonderful world in which we live. We see boulders which physical geographers say were made by great glaciers. Coal was formed out of buried trees and ferns; islands and reefs built up out of coral. In the study of geology, we learn about many of these forces that God used in building this universe. And the more we study, the more we realize anew that, yes, the creation of the universe required the mind of God *plus* the elements.

Evolution Cannot Explain Our Beginnings

Some people try to explain the fact of creation without God with a theory called "evolution." The dictionary tells us that "theory" means "an effort to explain something." But a theory is not a proven fact.

In trying to explain how Creation happened without God, evolutionary theory maintains that simple life started spontaneously from previously lifeless matter, and from this source all life came. Life then evolved or progressed into higher forms, so that man came from lower forms of life. But this is not what the Bible teaches.

A real problem for the biological evolutionist is this: apart from explaining the origin of life, *from what source did that first bit of matter come?* When the evolutionist has gone back as far as he can, he still must find the source of the first matter.

The Christian answer is: "In the beginning God created." Until God made it by the power of His Word, there was no matter.

Some theistic evolutionists (evolutionists who believe in God) believe that God did create the first bit of matter, but since then a process of evolution has been in effect. This position raises the question: Where is the relationship between the lowest forms of animal life and the highest forms of plant life? Where is the missing link between plants and animals?

Plants were created on the third day; animals on the sixth day (Genesis 1:11,12,24,31). *God's law is each kind "after his kind"* (Genesis 1:11,21,24). Apple trees always bring forth apples, never lemons. Apples come in many varieties, but they are always apples.

Luther Burbank bred better potatoes, but they were still potatoes. He crossed peaches and plums to produce nectarines, but botanically they are the same kind of fruit. Burbank could never have crossed peaches and pears, because they are of different species. Men may change and improve a species, but they cannot change one specie to another.

The late Dr. Robert Etheridge, a distinguished paleontologist with the British Museum, once commented that in that entire vast museum was not a single shred of evidence supporting the transmutation of species.

And Dr. George Howe, discussing some of the problems encountered by evolutionists, stated that—despite the claims of evolutionists—no fossils yet found confirm a relationship among the many forms of animal life. Each specie found in fossil form—whether a fish, a bat or a bird—appears already fully formed. He emphasized that the fossil record established no linkage between species.

Further, Dr. Howe emphasized that gene mutations or cell changes—a key point in the argument for evolution—are almost always harmful. Also, even if all the chmical elements essential to life existed in some primeval sea, stated Dr. Howe, the odds that even the most simple protein would arise without the creative action of God stagger the imagination.

Do you know that climbing beans always go up a pole from the left to the right? If a man reverses them they will die. It is not necessary to plant a seed right side up. God made each seed so that it always grows "up." Striped watermelons always have an even number of stripes. Citrus fruits always have an even number of sections. Ears of corn always have an even number of rows.

Would these rules be true if plants, animals, and men came about by accident?

God is the only Creator. He made all things Himself; He made this great unchanging law that each kind reproduces "after his kind."

"Who has measured the waters in the hollow of His hand, and marked off the heavens by the span, . . . and weighed the mountains in a balance, and the hills in a pair of scales?" (Isaiah 40:12).

"Lift up your eyes on high and see who has created these stars, the One who leads forth their host by number, He calls them all by name; because of the greatness of His might, and the strength of His power, not one of them is missing" (Isaiah 40:26).

"Do you not know? Have you not heard? The everlasting God, the Lord, the Creator of the ends of the earth does not become weary or tired. His understanding is inscrutable" (Isaiah 40:28).

Biological evolutionists say that between man and lower forms of life there is another missing link. If this link could be found, they think they could explain the theory of the evolution of man. However, this link will always be missing because it does not exist. From time to time various skeletal remains are discovered, but none is conclusive evidence that any is the long-sought missing link.

The late Dr. Edward Conklin, a professor of biology at Princeton University commented graphically about the evolutionist's belief in the accidental origin of life when he suggested that the likelihood of life originating in such a manner is as probable as an explosion in a printing plant resulting in an unabridged dictionary!

Of course, at one time no heaven and earth existed. There was only God. When heaven and earth were formed, God formed them. They did not happen into being; God made them. Everything that exists by creation God made. "For in him all things were created, both in the heavens and on the earth visible and invisible, whether thrones or dominions or rulers or authorities—all things have been created through him and for him" (Colossians 1:16).

The Beginning of Creation Genesis 1:1, 2

God began time with the creation of the heavens and earth. We do not have any record of how long God took to do this, and we cannot even attempt to estimate this. *One thing we do know is that God planned this earth to be our home and the training place for us as Christians. We know that God's children are more precious to Him than all of this world which He has created.*

"But happy is the man who has the God of Jacob as his helper, whose hope is in the Lord his God—the God who made both earth and heaven, the seas and everything in them. He is the God who keeps every promise" (Psalm 146:5,6). Yes, God existed long before this Creation and then He made it for us! "Before the mountains were brought forth, or ever thou hadst formed the earth and the world, even from everlasting to everlasting, thou art God" (Psalm 90:2).

Leading theologians and Christian scientists believe that Genesis 1:1 is an overall statement of the beginning of God's creation of the heavens and earth. They believe Genesis 1:2-31 is a progressive record of God's creation of the earth which simply continues from the beginning which was created in Genesis 1:1. Thus the statement "the earth was without form, and void" (Genesis 1:2) describes the first stage of God's creation of the earth according to this group of people. They believe that the earth was in a gaseous or fluid condition in Genesis 1:1.

The climax of all creation is man. God did not create man until He had prepared a place for him. We may think that we are not very important when we look at the vastness of this universe. Yet man, we are told, was made in God's image. He can think God's thoughts after Him. He can do God's will. He can respond to God's love. Therefore, God has built this world to be man's dwelling place.

We need to be careful and not be self-confident or judgmental in our attitudes toward others who may take a somewhat different view of how God created the earth in Genesis 1:1,2. If we accept the authority of the Bible as God's Word, we need to be very cautious and careful in forming our own conclusions and perhaps even set aside some of our questions on Creation until we meet God in heaven where He can clearly tell us exactly what He did in Genesis 1:1,2. God has chosen to keep these details partially veiled from us as human beings.

The Bible says, "Where were you when I laid the foundation of the earth! Tell Me, if you have understanding, who set its measurements, since you know? Or who stretched the line on it? On what were its bases sunk? Or who laid its cornerstone, when the morning stars sang together, and all the sons of God shouted for joy?" (Job 38:4-7). (See Isaiah 48:13, Isaiah 45:7 and 12, Jeremiah 32:17.)

Consider the phrase in Genesis 1:2: "the Spirit of God" moved over the face of the water. The Holy Spirit is one of the three persons of the Godhead; each one has a distinct personality and yet all are One. The Holy Spirit should never be spoken of as "it" but as a person, as "He."

Just as the Holy Spirit "moved" over the face of the deep, the Holy Spirit moves and works upon those who do not know Jesus Christ. He shows us from God's Word just how much God loves us. And by putting faith into our hearts, He encourages us to respond to

25

God's love by receiving His Son, the Lord Jesus Christ.

Have you ever experienced the moving of the Holy Spirit upon your heart and invited Jesus Christ to be your Lord and Savior? This could be the creative work which God wants to do in your life today. If you have done this, have you experienced the moving of the Holy Spirit in your life asking you to yield your life fully to the Lord Jesus Christ to be used in whatever way you are needed? (Romans 12:1-2). Why not stop now, consider these matters and respond as you feel the Holy Spirit moving in your life in one of these areas?

The First Day: Light Genesis 1:3-5

As God spoke, the darkness was dispelled by the light. God separated light from darkness, for light and darkness cannot mix. Think of all the different kinds of light you know—sunlight, gas, oil, electric, candle, fire, match, lightning bug, glowworm, etc. All these lights trace back to the sunshine and God. The coal in the hill only stores up the sunshine which our furnaces release for us. "Every good gift and every perfect gift is from above" (James 1:17).

Notice that there is no mention of any means used in Creation by God, except His Word. There is only the simple statement of the fact "and it was so."

God has many promises in His Word for us today. He has spoken them and holy men have recorded them in the Bible for us. Because God has made these promises, He will be faithful to His Word and complete working them out in our lives.

Do you underline the promises of God in your Bible? This is a good habit to form. Following are some promises which you might want to underline in your Bible today:

Psalm 3:3: "But thou, O Lord, art a shield for me; my glory, and the lifter up of mine head."

Psalm 50:15: "Call upon me in the day of trouble: I will deliver thee, and thou shalt glorify me."

Second Peter 2:9: "The Lord knoweth how to deliver the godly out of temptations."

First Peter 3:12: "The eyes of the Lord are over the righteous, and his ears are open unto their prayers."

The Second Day Genesis 1:6-8

Here we find that God divided the waters. The firmament was made by the separation of the salt waters beneath and the fresh waters above. Here is another mystery which the human cannot fully comprehend. We see great cloud chariots floating overhead carrying tons

26

of water. *What keeps them up there? Why don't they drop?* God *just spoke* and there the water hangs until He is ready to have it come down and bless the earth in the form of raindrops! God established the natural law that makes all of this possible.

The purpose of Creation is the preparation of a home for man. The world was made for man to enjoy. His needs from the animal and vegetable world had been provided, before he was created. How wonderful that the light, the heat, the moisture, and the earth, essential for plant and animal life, came first. This reveals to us that God is infinite in wisdom and power and is infinite in His love to us. What we owe Him! What could we do without Him?

In Job we find this question: "Dost thou know the balancings of the clouds?" (Job 37:16). Just think of what wonderful balancing this must be. Thousands of tons of water hang suspended in the sky. Certainly only God can do anything as wonderful as balancing clouds! Since He is able to do this, think of how perfectly He is able to bring everything in your life into proper balance by the power of His love for you! Will you trust God with your life today?

The Third Day Genesis 1:9-13

The land appeared as it emerged from beneath the water. The dry land made plant life possible, the fruit tree yielding fruit after its own kind. This is the law of growth that God established and it has been so ever since. You do not look for apples on a pear tree. You do not plant carrots and expect potatoes. God said "after his kind" (Genesis 1:11). Each thing that God created was to reproduce "after his kind."

In regard to day 3, Dr. George Howe reminds us that evolutionists believe seed-bearing plants evolved many millions of years *after* fish did. Yet the Bible here makes very clear that such plants were created on day 3 *before* God created fish.

Here is a place where the Bible makes good scientific sense and where the Bible writer corrects the errors of scientists "so-called." Nature shows a downward tendency. Retrogression of species certainly is well established. God made so many types of plants that even at this time there are about two hundred and fifty thousand species. God made desert plants, called belly plants, so small that only the

27

trained eye ever sees them. And yet these plants bloom with a beauty that is amazing. There is a desert calical flower which has petals of white, pink, and purple, yet the entire blossom is less than two-tenths of an inch across. The Rock Gila has such tiny flowers that the insects cannot get inside of them. Only God could make such delicate blossoms.

By comparison, God made the massive redwoods of Northern California. These are the largest trees in the world. One of them, the General Sherman, is nearly two hundred and eighty feet tall. It takes about twenty people with outstretched arms to reach around the trunk. When the Lord Jesus Christ was here on earth, this tree was about two thousand years old. Surely only God could make such a tree.

In Genesis 1:12 God looks at His creation and says that it is "good." The Hebrew word from which this word is translated actually means "beautiful." God is totally satisfied and delighted with His creation: He enjoys and delights in it.

Do you appreciate the wonders of God's creation as you look out over the world? Do you stop and thank God when you see beauty in nature? Do you help others to see and appreciate this beauty? Why not make it a point this week to be more thankful to God for the beauty of His creation?

The Fourth Day Genesis 1:14-19

The two great lights for the earth were set for seasons, days, and years. The sun is nearly ninety-three million miles away from the earth. The temperature on its surface is about twelve thousand degrees F. If the sun were closer, life on the earth would be impossible. If it were farther away, the earth would be too cold for life. God put the sun in just the right place.

The sun is about eight hundred and sixty-five thousand miles in diameter—not a very large body as stars go. It appears so bright because it is so close to the earth. If it were as far away as the stars in the Big Dipper are, we could not see it without a telescope. The star, Betelgeuse, in the constellation Orion is more than a million times as big as the sun. God created the sun, moon, and stars by just His words "let there be lights in the firmament" (Genesis 1:14).

When we look at the vastness of the universe, we wonder, "Does the Creator of all things know or care about me?" We feel like David when he said, "When I consider thy heavens, the work of thy fingers, the moon and the stars, which thou hast ordained; what is man, that thou art mindful of him?" (Psalm 8:3,4). Yet, we know that David knew that God did care for him. Read Psalm 23 to know how David expressed God's care for him.

God takes care of us, too. He does want to lead and guide us. The question is not with God; the question is with us. Do we want God to lead us? Are you willing to follow when God tells you what He wants you to do this week? Ask yourself what God would have you do this week. Pray that His Holy Spirit will reveal His plan to you.

The Fifth Day: The Creation of Living Things Genesis 1:20-23

This passage tells us of the creation of animal life in the water and in the air. Again God says that each is to bring forth "after his kind." God created fish that range in size from a tiny minnow to a great whale. The whale is the largest living animal that man has ever seen, larger even than the prehistoric monsters. The main artery of the whale is a pipe large enough to easily hold a full-grown man!

God made birds to fly in the heavens. Lightness and buoyancy were, of course, important. The great Creator knew this and He made the bones of the birds so that they may be filled with air as a sponge is filled with water. In fact the whole body is inflated like a balloon. Even the feathers which cover the birds are marvelous examples of ingenuity. Each feather is a series of amazing locks, as many as a million per large feather. These locks hold the feather together. If the feather is torn, the bird "preens" it back together again.

The Sixth Day Genesis 1:24-31

There were a great many things that God made on the sixth day of Creation. The Bible says that all the creeping things were made. Do you know that for each of the stars which you can see on a clear night God has created a hundred different species of insects?

On the sixth day, too, animals and man were created. The climax of all creation is man. *God did not create man until He had prepared a place for him.* We may think that we are not very important when we look at the vastness of this universe. Yet man, we are told, was made in God's image. He can think God's thoughts after Him. He can do God's will. He can respond to God's love. Therefore, God has built this world to be man's dwelling place.

Genesis 1:26 says, "Let us make man in our image." Really the purpose of Creation is the preparation of a home for man. The world was made for man to enjoy. His needs from the animal and vegetable world had been provided, before he was created. How wonderful that the light, the heat, the moisture, and the earth, essential for plant and animal life, came first. This reveals to us that God is infinite in wisdom and power and is infinite in His love to us. What we owe Him! What could we do without Him?

When all things were ready, then the Lord God made man. The Bible describes the creation of man like this: "So God created man in his own image, in the image of God created he him" (Genesis 1:27). And again, "And the Lord God formed man of the dust of the ground, and breathed into his nostrils the breath of life; and man became a living soul" (Genesis 2:7). The dust here must be a real substance as the same word appears in such a context in Genesis 3:19 that would prevent any other rendering.

Theistic evolutionists argue that dust means our animal ancestor. However, the Scriptures give absolutely no indication of this theory. The rest of the Creation God made by the word of His power, but man was made in a special way. And then, God breathed life into him. This is not said of any other of God's creations. At the beginning God gave man a position which he could never attain unto by himself.

When God created man, He gave him "dominion." Let us make a list right now of things over which man must rule (Genesis 1:28). The earth yields to us precious treasure at God's bidding. Grain and fruit grow. Animals become obedient to our commands. They also serve as food. The seas, rivers, and lakes carry our ships. They turn water wheels to make electricity for us. They give us water to drink. The sun warms us and lights our way; it puts life into corn and wheat so that they may grow.

Surely we see God's goodness and love toward us in all these things. God created this beautiful world to meet all of our physical needs and for our enjoyment. He expects us to rule it properly as everything He made was very good (Genesis 1:31).

God has revealed Himself as a living person in His creation. We see His love for us all around us in this world. God made us to have fellowship with Himself. "Behold, I stand at the door, and knock: if any man hear my voice, and open the door, I will come in to him, and will sup with him, and he with me" (Revelation 3:20).

Study Questions

Before you begin your study this week:
1. Pray and ask God to speak to you through His Holy Spirit each day.
2. Use only your Bible for your answers.
3. Write your answers and the verses you have used.
4. Challenge questions are for those who have the time and wish to do them.
5. Personal questions are to be shared with your study group only if you wish to share.
6. As you study look for a verse to memorize this week. Write it down, carry it with you, tack it to your bulletin board, tape it to the dashboard of your car. Make a real effort to learn the verse and its reference.

FIRST DAY: Read all of the notes and look up all of the Scriptures.

1. What was a helpful or new thought from the overview of Genesis 1?

2. What personal application did you select to apply to your own life this week?

SECOND DAY: Read all of Genesis 2, concentrating on verses 1-4.

1 a. When heaven, earth, and all that they contained were completed, what did God do on the seventh day?

 b. What did God instruct the Jewish people to do on the seventh day according to Exodus 23:12?

 c. What principle of rest is even suggested for the land in Exodus 23:10,11? How often does God say this should be done?

31

2 a. What does Jesus Christ suggest that His apostles do after they have had a busy time teaching and working for the Lord? See Mark 6:30-32.

   b. Do you believe that God wants you to draw apart and rest from daily activities so that you can have fellowship with Him and enjoy Him?

   c. (Personal) Do you and your family set aside Sunday as a special day of rest to enjoy the Lord and worship Him?

   d. What are some ways in which you could make Sunday a day of rest and worship and a special, joyous day?

3 a. According to Mark 16:9, what day was it when Jesus Christ rose from the dead?

   b. If the last day of the week is Saturday (Sabbath), what name do we give the first day of the week?

4. When did the disciples of the Lord Jesus come together for communion and a time of preaching and worship according to Acts 20:7?

5. **Challenge:** Though Isaiah 58:13,14 is speaking of the blessing of God on the Jewish people who would keep the Sabbath laws, read and relate it to the Christian's keeping of Sunday. Put these verses in your own words as you write them here.

6 a. What does Psalm 122:1 say?

b. (Personal) Do you have this emotion when Sunday comes? If not, pray and ask God to put this desire in your heart.

THIRD DAY: Read Genesis 2:5-7.

1. Was there any rain on the earth at first?

2. How was the soil watered at this time?

3. What do you find different about the creation of man compared to all of the other things God created in Genesis 1? See Genesis 1 with Genesis 2:7.

4. Of all of the Creation, man was the only one created as a trinity. What does 1 Thessalonians 5:23 say man consists of?

5. **Challenge:** God created us to have fellowship with Him. As we read His Word, the Bible, and pray daily, the Lord will guide us continually. Read Isaiah 58:11 and put the thoughts in this verse in your own words.

6 a. Read Revelation 22:17. Who do you think the water of life is in this verse? What do John 4:10 and John 7:37 say concerning the water of life?

b. (Personal) Have you ever thirsted for the water of life? The Lord Jesus Christ offers Himself to you. He wants to give you living water.

c. What does 2 Timothy 1:9,10 say concerning what the Lord Jesus Christ has done for those who place their faith in Him? Note that this was planned before the world was created!

FOURTH DAY: Genesis 2:8-17.

1. Where did God put man after He created him?

2 a. What kind of trees did God cause to grow in Eden?

b. What did God water the Garden of Eden with?

c. Name the four heads of the river and where they flowed.

d. **Challenge:** How do you see God's love for man expressed in Genesis 2:8-14?

3 a. What was man's work in the garden?

b. (Personal) What do you believe the work is that God has planned for you in your world and your church?

34

4 a. What one thing did God ask Adam to be obedient in?

   b. (Personal) Are there things in your life which God has asked you
      to refrain from doing in obedience to the Holy Spirit's leading?
      Have you been obedient to God in this? Please share with your
      discussion group your thoughts about this, if possible.

5. Do you believe that God has provided us with a tree of life (Genesis 2:9) today? What do John 14:6 and John 6:40 say about this?

   John 14:6

   John 6:40

6 a. The New Testament speaks of the death which comes to those
     who refuse the "tree of life," Jesus Christ. Put into your own
     words what the following verses say concerning this.

     John 3:36

     Romans 6:23

   b. (Personal) Have you received Jesus Christ and the life He prom-
      ises? See Revelation 3:20.

FIFTH DAY: Genesis 2:18-25.

1 What did God make woman to be?

35

2 a. Who brought the animals and fowl to Adam so that he could name them?

   b. **Challenge:** Do you see God's fellowship and love for Adam expressed in Genesis 2:19?

   c. (Personal) Have you recognized that God created you for fellowship with Him? If you are lonely, frustrated, and lacking in confidence, remember this! Talk aloud to God and thank Him for His love toward you. Ask Him to help you to remember His love when you have loneliness in your life.

3 a. Describe how God created the "help meet" for Adam in Genesis 2:21, 22.

   b. How did Adam describe Eve, and what did he name her?

4. What is said about woman in Genesis 2:24?

5. The greatest of all contracts is marriage. Today many who wouldn't think of dishonoring a contract in business are dishonoring their marriage contract which unites the man to the wife by the Lord. What does Malachi 2:13-16 say concerning this subject?

6. What does Ephesians 5:25 say concerning the husband's love for the wife?

SIXTH DAY: Read the following related scriptures concerning marriage and put them into your own words.

1. Proverbs 18:22

   Proverbs 21:9 and Proverbs 21:19

   Mark 10:2-9

   Proverbs 31:10-31

   Colossians 3:18,19

2. Which of these verses do you feel is most important in our day?

3. (Personal) Was there a message in any of these verses that you would like to apply to your life and trust God by the Holy Spirit to work out in your life? Be specific. See Philippians 2:13. What encouragement do you find here concerning this?

4. Which verse in this lesson did you choose to memorize? Why did you choose it?

MAN AND WOMAN: GOD'S SPECIAL CREATIVE ACT

GENESIS 2

Study Notes

God led Moses by the Holy Spirit to write the Pentateuch (the first five books of the Bible). *The Lord Jesus Christ spoke of Moses writing these books (John 5:45-47).* Man has put the chapter divisions into Moses' writings, not God. These divisions were made for the purpose of reference and study only. Therefore, we need to consider Genesis 1 and Genesis 2 as one total account of God's creation. *Chapter 2 merely complements and adds detail to chapter 1. There is no contradiction of one or the other.*

Both chapters begin at different places in the creation process. Genesis 1 begins with a watery chaos and Genesis 2 begins to give us the details of the dry earth which God created in the second day (Genesis 1:6-8). Thus we see that Genesis 2 is simply a more detailed account of Genesis 1.

A husband might come home and ask his wife what she has done during the day, and she would reply, "I went downtown and did some shopping." Later the wife might tell her husband that while she was downtown she met a friend and had lunch with her. *The second account would not contradict the first statement, but would be a detailed story of the same thing.*

Some critics say that in Genesis 2 God created the vegetation after He created man. However, the creation of vegetation is described in Genesis 1:9-13. God did not create vegetation in Genesis 2, but simply planted a garden (Genesis 2:8).

Others criticize Genesis 2:19 where God brought the animals to Adam, saying it contradicts Genesis 1:20-23 where God created the animals on the fifth day. When we read Genesis 2:19 we discover that God formed the animals out of the ground and brought them to Adam to see what he would call them. This was simply an enlargement of how God created the animals as given to us in Genesis 1, and then the explanation of how God brought them to Adam to be named.

An interesting observation is that the verbs used in Genesis 2:8,9 and 19 imply the pluperfect tense. The pluperfect tense expresses a past time prior to some other past time, according to the standard dictionary definition. Thus the verb in Genesis 2:8,9 refers to God planting previously created plants in the Garden of Eden and the verb in Genesis 2:19 refers to previously created beasts being brought to Adam now for him to name.

Archaeology Confirms Our Bible

Reports from archaeologists confirm the truth of these ancient writings concerning the origin and fall of Adam and Eve. On some of the most ancient tablets dug up in Babylon, it is stated, "Near Eridu (Eden) was a garden in which was a mysterious sacred tree . . . of life, planted by the gods . . . and protected by two guardian spirits so that no man dare enter into the midst of it." (Compare this with Genesis 3:23,24.)

Genesis 2:8 states that after God created Adam and Eve, He placed them in "a garden eastward in Eden." This region, in which the garden must have been located, can be identified with some accuracy, since several rivers are specified as being in the vicinity (Genesis 2:10-14). Two of these rivers, the Euphrates and the Hiddekel (an ancient name for the Tigris) are still known. Both rise in Armenia, (now eastern Turkey), and their headwaters are only a few miles apart. They run together, about one hundred miles north of the Persian Gulf. Monuments in ancient Babylon mention that the city near the fountainhead of these rivers was "Eridu," the world's oldest and most sacred site.

Dr. G. Coleman Luck wrote some years ago that two ancient seals had been discovered bearing witness to the record of the temptation of Adam and Eve. One was found at a strata level going back before 3000 B.C. and showing an unclothed man and woman walking about as if downcast. Following them was a serpent. The other seal, found in Nineveh, depicts a tree with a man on the right side and a woman on the left side. The woman is picking fruit, and behind her is an erect serpent which appears to be speaking to her. Thus archaeology confirms that there was widespread knowledge of the main features of the Genesis account well over 5000 years ago!

It is also interesting to note what missionaries to remote jungle tribes have to say. *These tribes always have a remnant of the Creation story and of the Great Flood* (Genesis 6—9). Though they have had no previous contact with white men these stories have been preserved by word of mouth from one tribal chieftain to the next through the years.

The exact site of the Garden of Eden is not known. The important point to remember is that archaeological research has proved that the basin of the eastern Mediterranean where these two rivers still exist and the region immediately to the east of this basin is, without any doubt, the cradle of civilization.

God Rests Genesis 2:1-3

The Bible says, "Thus the heavens and the earth were completed, and all their hosts. And by the seventh day God completed His work which He had done; and He rested on the seventh day from all His work which He had done" (Genesis 2:1-3). *This passage does not mean that God was tired; it means that God had completed His work of creation and now He took time to enjoy it.*

Do you feel lonely, lack self-confidence, or are you unhappy in your present situation? Remember that God created you to have fellowship with Him; He loves you. Pray aloud to God and ask Him to help you in whatever your problem is. He is always waiting to hear from you and wants to help you today.

In Genesis 2:3 God "blessed the seventh day, and sanctified it." God blessed the day of rest and set it apart as a special day; that means He set it apart from the other days of the week. As God looked at the universe which He had created, He saw "all that he had made, and, behold, it was very good" (Genesis 1:31). God then rested from His work to enjoy the smallest flower, the largest animal, and the largest star in the heaven.

God set a pattern in this example for us. He intends for us to work six days and to rest on the seventh. We are to enjoy God and His creation on this day of rest. We are to worship Him and thank Him for all of the blessings which He has given to us.

In Genesis 1:28 we read "and God blessed them (man and woman)." What does the word "blessed" mean to you? To be blessed is to be made happy by God's love and goodness to us and by the presence of God in our lives. We are to enjoy God every day of our lives, but one day is to be set apart as a special day to concentrate particularly on worshiping Him.

The "Sabbath" was to remind every human being of the coming rest which Christ would bring when He came to earth and died on the cross to forgive us our sins. "Having made peace through the blood of His cross; through Him, I say, whether things on earth or things in heaven. And although you were formerly alienated and hostile in mind, engaged in evil deeds, yet He has now reconciled you in His fleshly body through death, in order to present you before him holy and blameless and beyond reproach" (Colossians 1:20-22).

The Jewish people kept the seventh day, the Sabbath. *The Lord Jesus arose on the first day of the week (Mark 16:9) and therefore it was this day the first Christians kept as their day of rest carrying out the principle which God established in Genesis 2:3 (Acts 20:7).* Thus they deliberately chose the day which symbolized their freedom of guilt from sin, the resurrection of Jesus Christ, to set aside their work and enter into the joy of God through Jesus Christ.

Have you chosen to spend this day with Him? A special blessing is promised to those who choose to follow God's plan in this practice (Isaiah 58:13,14). We are promised delight in the Lord and also we will "ride on the heights of the earth."

Have you chosen to make Sunday a special day in your life and in the life of your family? Do you seek to please God by resting and worshiping Him on this day? Sunday should be a delightful day for all. Our attitude and preparation is the key to this delight. If we delight ourselves in the Lord, He will take us to "high places" of great joy in fellowship with Him. He has promised it.

Are your children learning about the love of the Lord Jesus Christ by listening to your loving words and acts, not only through the week, but on this special day of Sunday? Are they learning to say, "I was glad when they said unto me, Let us go into the house of the Lord" (Psalm 122:1)?

God Plants the Garden of Eden. Further Details on the Creation of Adam
Genesis 2:4-7

In Genesis 1 we see the name "God" used, but as we move into Genesis 2:4 we find God called "Lord God." *The name God (Elohim) especially refers to God as Creator;* this is why it is used in Genesis 1 particularly. Now we find the name "Lord" (*Jehovah*) added to the name God the Creator. Jehovah is the Hebrew for "I Am." *The word Jehovah (Lord) is the name God uses for Himself when He wants to remind us of His love and care.* He is to people whatever their need is.

Do you feel lonely, lack self-confidence, or are you unhappy in your present situation? Remember that God created you to have fellowship with Him; He loves you. Pray aloud to God and ask Him to help you in whatever your problem is. He is always waiting to hear from you and wants to help you today.

In Genesis 2:7 we are given *further details* of how the Lord God created man from the dust of the ground and then breathed into his nostrils the breath of life; thus man became a living soul. In Genesis 1:26 we read "And God said, Let us make man in *our* image." *God is a trinity indicated by the word "our"* (God the Father, God the Son, and God the Holy Spirit). Read Titus 3:4-6; Hebrews 9:14; and 1 Peter 1:2.

Adam and Eve were created innocent; God gave them the power to choose between right and wrong. They did not have to choose right, and they did not have to choose to do wrong. They had a free will. They could do as they chose. God wanted them to obey Him, but He gave them the right to choose to obey. He did not make them obey. The Lord gives us the same power of choice.

The Spirit gives man a God-consciousness that no animal has. There has never been an altar built to God by an animal. Man was created in the image of God; God has emotions of love (Deuteronomy 7:7,8,13; John 3:16); of joy (Zephaniah 3:17; John 15:11); of peace (1 Corinthians 14:33; Colossians 3:15). God also thinks (Isaiah 55:8); God also hates evil (Proverbs 8:13). Just as God experiences these emotions, He created us to experience these same emotions.

God also has the power of a free will to determine what He chooses to do (Deuteronomy 12:5,11,14,18,26; 1 Corinthians 1:27). *God also created man with a free will* (Joshua 24:15; Philippians 1:22). *We either choose to obey God or to disobey Him.* "Choose for yourselves today whom you will serve" (Joshua 24:15).

Man was created in the image of God on the sixth day. In Genesis 2:19 we are reminded that God created the animals from the ground. But there is also the reminder in Genesis 2:7 that man is very different though there are many close resemblances in physical organs and frame to the animals. Man alone was created in the likeness of God (Genesis 1:27) and actually had the breath of God breathed into him so that he would become a living soul (Genesis 2:7). Man is the climax

43

of God's creation. All of the rest God created for man to enjoy and have dominion over.

The Garden of Eden Genesis 2:8-17

The Lord God planted a garden in Eden. There He put the man whom He had created. God's love is seen in His provision of trees that were not only good for food, but those that were pleasant to the sight (Genesis 2:9). The word "Eden" means a park and a place of happiness. *God's love personally arranged the beauty here for Adam.*

God also deliberately put the Tree of Life and the Tree of Knowledge of Good and Evil in this garden. The Tree of Life was not forbidden to Adam until after he had sinned (Genesis 2:16). It probably was a real tree with real fruit on it. God meant it to be a type of the Lord Jesus Christ who alone gives life. Jesus said of Himself in John 14:6: "I am the way, and the truth, and the life; no one comes to the Father, but through Me." Have you come by way of Jesus Christ to God the Father? Are you helping others to find the Lord Jesus Christ who is our "Tree of Life"?

The Tree of the Knowledge of Good and Evil was forbidden to man (Genesis 2:17). The tree was to test the obedience of Adam and his future wife Eve! It probably was a real tree, since the test was real and the results were real. Probably the fruit was no different from any other fruit on the trees in the Garden of Eden.

The sin was not in the fruit but in the choice of being disobedient to God. Adam and Eve were created innocent; God gave them the power to choose between right and wrong. They did not have to choose right, and they did not have to choose to do wrong. They had a free will. They could do as they chose. *God wanted them to obey Him, but He gave them the right to choose to obey. He did not make them obey.*

The Lord gives us the same power of choice. We are not asked to choose whether to eat of the fruit of a certain tree, but we are faced with choices. God does not make us obey Him. He asks us to obey Him, and leaves the choice up to us.

We are faced with many choices every day, but the greatest choice concerns the Lord Jesus Christ. Will you decide for Christ, or against Him? The consequences of this choice are very plain. If you decide against Christ, you will be barred from heaven forever (Matthew 10:32,33). But if you decide for Him you will become God's child and you will have heaven for your eternal home (John 3:36). Have you made your choice for God?

As Christians we have other choices to make. Will we walk according to God's plan for our lives, or will we go our own way? "In every-

44

thing you do, put God first, and he will direct you and crown your efforts with success" (Proverbs 3:6). "Tell me where you want me to go and I will go there. May every fiber of my being unite in reverence to your name" (Psalm 86:11). Psalm 86:11 should be the Christian's prayer. Is this your prayer today?

Many years ago Patrick Henry made a great choice. He said, "Give me liberty or give me death." He preferred death to slavery. He made his choice. If you are a Christian, you have made the greatest choice—Jesus Christ as your Savior.

But every day you are faced with more choices. Make your choice only when you are sure that what you decide will please your Lord and Savior. Seek His plan for your life daily in prayer and in the study of the Bible. Joy of Living Bible Study has provided a daily plan for you so that you can seek His will in your life. Then when you know what the right choice is, do it!

God put man in the Garden of Eden to dress it and keep it (Genesis 2:15). This word "man" in the original Hebrew is Adam and means man. God gave Adam work to do in order to keep him happy. A person who is happily absorbed in work finds fulfillment in it. God established this as a principle in the Garden of Eden when He had Adam cultivate the garden and keep or guard it.

Are you happy in your present work, and do you see it as God's gift to you for the total development of your personality? What work has God given you to do in this world? What work has God given you to do in your church? God has planned a work for each of us to do. Pray and ask God what your work is in this world and in His Church.

Do you feel overworked, strained, and under tension? Many in our society today do. God has recorded a promise for you in Matthew 11:28-30. Jesus said these words, "Come to me and I will give you rest—all of you who work so hard beneath a heavy yoke. Wear my yoke—for it fits perfectly—and let me teach you; for I am gentle and humble, and you shall find rest for your souls; for I give you only light burdens." Your daily work will be a great joy and fulfillment as you are yoked together with Jesus Christ!

Before leaving this section, note that Adam was told to keep the Garden of Eden or to guard it. There were no thorns; nor was there any bad soil to frustrate Adam. His work was without tension or strain. God wants our homes to be places where there are no thorns or bad soil.

What do you do to guard your home against the entrance of enemies? There are many enemies in this world which attempt to invade our homes and bring tension and strain to us. The wrong kind of literature, the wrong type of television program, the wrong kind of music are some of the influences which may be invading your life or your home. Pray and ask God to show you where the thorns and bad soil are in your home and in your life. Ask Him to give you the power to remove them from your life so that you can avoid the strain and tension they bring.

"But remember this—the wrong desires that come into your life aren't anything new and different. Many others have faced exactly the same problems before you. *And no temptation is irresistible. You can trust God to keep the temptation from becoming so strong that you can't stand up against it,* for he has promised this, and will do what he says. He will show you how to escape temptation's power so that you can bear up patiently against it" (1 Corinthians 10:13, italics added). Will you rely on God to do this in your life?

The Creation of Eve Genesis 2:18-25

God planned for Adam to have dominion over the whole earth, and therefore He brought each of the animals to Adam for him to name (Genesis 2:19). We see God's love for Adam as He had fellowship with Adam and brought the animals to him for naming. Think of the capacity God gave Adam to name these animals as this project was undertaken. As God brought these animals to Adam, Adam began to recognize that there was a great gulf between himself and the most manlike animal such as the ape. Adam discovered that there was a deep desire within himself for human companionship, for we read in Genesis 2:20, "But for Adam there was not found a help meet."

The Lord God caused a deep sleep to come upon Adam and then God took one of Adam's ribs from which He made woman. Because she is made of the same flesh, she is called "woman." Matthew Henry said, "The woman was formed out of man—not out of his head to rule over him; not out of his feet to be trod upon by him; but out of his side to be his equal, from beneath his arm to be protected, and from near his heart to be loved."[1] Adam needed this companionship not only for sexual reproduction so that they could replenish the earth, but also to develop him socially and for encouragement in taking proper care of God's earth.

Man and woman became one flesh in marriage (Matthew 19:5; Mark 10:7,8; Ephesians 5:31). The love of the husband and the wife is to be lasting as God's love is for us. All through the Old Testament God compares His love for His people to the love of a husband for his wife (Isaiah 62:5; Hosea 2:19,20). And in the New Testament, the Lord Jesus is portrayed as the Bridegroom of the Church which is bone "of his bones" (Ephesians 5:25-33; Revelation 21:9).

Woman is to be a permanent companion of man as they come together in marriage. Today, the contract of marriage has been dealt

46

often with dishonor. Many who honor business contracts dishonor the marriage contract. Malachi 2:15-16 has words of wisdom for us, "Therefore guard your passions! Keep faith with the wife of your youth. For the Lord, the God of Israel, says he hates divorce."

Marriage is not to be entered into lightly. God planned for marriage to last until "death do us part." Pray and ask God to help you to follow His guidelines concerning marriage which you find in the Scriptures (Ephesians 5:25; Proverbs 18:22; Mark 10:2-9). Marriage in God's sight involves spiritual, mental, and physical oneness. As you realize this, are you teaching your children the importance of Christian marriage? Are you sharing these Scriptures on marriage with them?

NOTE

1. Sherwood Eliot Wirt and Kersten Beckstrom, *Living Quotations for Christians* (New York: Harper & Row, Publishers, 1974), p. 357.

Study Questions

Before you begin this week:
1. Pray and ask God to speak to you through His Holy Spirit each day.
2. Use only your Bible for your answers.
3. Write your answers and the verses you have used.
4. Challenge questions are for those who have the time and wish to do them.
5. Personal questions are to be shared with your study group only if you wish to share.
6. As you study look for a verse to memorize this week. Write it down, carry it with you, tack it to your bulletin board, tape it to the dashboard of your car. Make a real effort to learn the verse and its reference.

FIRST DAY: Read all of the notes and look up all of the Scriptures.

1. What was a helpful or new thought from the overview of Genesis 2?

2. What personal application did you select to apply to your own life this week?

SECOND DAY: Read all of Genesis 3, concentrating on Genesis 3:1-3.

1. How was the serpent described in Genesis 3:1?

2. Read Revelation 12:9 and Revelation 20:2. What are two of the serpent's names?

3. **Challenge:** Where is Satan's dwelling place now? Summarize in your own words the following verses about this.

48

Luke 10:18

2 Corinthians 4:4

Revelation 12:9-12

Job 1:7

4. The serpent, Satan, is described in Genesis 3:1. His character is described in many other places in the Bible. Pick out the key thoughts about Satan from the following verses:

1 Peter 5:8

1 John 2:13

Acts 5:3

John 8:44

5. **Challenge:** What warnings and commands are we given in the Bible about adding to God's Word or removing something from God's Word?

Deuteronomy 4:2

Deuteronomy 12:32

Proverbs 30:5,6

Revelation 22:18

6 a. Compare how Eve quoted God in Genesis 3:3 with Genesis
2:17 where God gave directions concerning the Tree of the
Knowledge of Good and Evil. What is different in Genesis 3:3?

    b. (Personal) Do you receive all of God's Word as His truth? Have
you ever considered adding to it some of men's writings? Have
you ever taken away part of His Word because you didn't agree
with it?

THIRD DAY: Read Genesis 3:4-6 with Ephesians 6.

1. Challenge: How does Genesis 3:4,5 tie in with John 8:44?

2. What do the following verses suggest Eve could have done and
thus remain obedient to God's command not to eat of the fruit of
the Tree of Knowledge?

Ephesians 4:27

James 4:7

3. How do the following verses encourage you, as they speak of the Lord Jesus Christ's help and final victory over the devil?

Romans 16:20

Colossians 1:13

1 John 4:4

1 John 5:4,5

4   Read Ephesians 6:10-18, which speaks of the protection God provides for the one who has received His Son by faith.

   a. Where do we receive our strength to stand against Satan's subtle wiles?

   b. Use the descriptive words that express what God's armor is. Example: gird your loins—with truth.

   c. Does prayer have anything to do with God's protection from Satan?

d. (Personal) Have you done what Ephesians 6:18 tells you to do? Read John 3:16-18 concerning faith.

5 a. How did Satan make the tree appear to Eve so that she would eat according to Genesis 3:6?

b. (Personal) Do you believe that Satan tempts us in the same ways today? What are some temptations you can think of that are similar today?

6. What is the purpose of any temptation of Satan today, according to 2 Corinthians 11:3?

FOURTH DAY: Read Genesis 3:7-19.

1. What was the result of Adam and Eve's disobedience to God according to Genesis 3:7?

2 a. What does Romans 3:23 tell us about mankind since the time of Adam and Eve?

b. What are the wages of sin, and what is the gift of God through Jesus Christ? See Romans 6:23.

c. (Personal) Have you received this gift for yourself yet? How are you sharing this wonderful gift with others?

3 a. Who did Adam blame for his sin, and who did Eve blame? (Give verse.)

 b. How does Psalm 32:5 show us that we need to be honest with God in naming our sins? Put this Psalm into your own words as though you personally are speaking to God concerning these things.

 c. How does 1 John 1:9 complement the thoughts in Psalm 32:5?

4. (Personal) Have you prayed today, thanked God for His blessings, and named your sins and asked Him to forgive them for Jesus' sake? Why not stop right now and talk with the Lord?

5. What was the curse that God put on the serpent because of what he had done? See Genesis 3:14,15.

6. Summarize the other curses relating to this situation. (Give verses.)

 Eve's

 Adam's

 Soil

Death in the world

FIFTH DAY: Read Genesis 3:20-24.

1. **Challenge:** Study Genesis 3:16 with Ephesians 5:21-32. How does the Lord Jesus Christ set a pattern of love and honor as He heads the church? This is to be an example to the Christian couple.

2. Why did Adam call his wife Eve?

3. What did God clothe Adam and Eve in?

4. What had to die in order that they could be "covered" in their nakedness caused by sin?

5 a. What does Psalm 32:1 say about sins that are "covered"?

   b. According to 1 John 1:7, what cleanses us from all sin?

   c. Who chose to die for us in order that our sins could be "covered" and forgiven?

6. Where did God put Adam and Eve after their disobedience, and how did He guard the Garden of Eden?

SIXTH DAY: Read Matthew 4:1-11 concerning the devil's temptation of Jesus Christ.

1. What was different about the place where Jesus Christ was
   tempted, compared to where Adam and Eve were tempted?

2. What was Jesus Christ doing before the temptation?

3 a. **Challenge:** Satan tempted the Lord Jesus three times. What
   was Jesus' weapon each time against the temptation?

   b. (Personal) Do you believe that you have this same weapon available to you today? Do you use it?

4. Are you doing what Psalm 119:11 suggests?

5. What did Jesus Christ say in Matthew 4:10 which we can say, too?

6 a. When the devil left the Lord Jesus, who ministered to Him?

   b. Read Hebrews 1:7, Hebrews 1:14, and Hebrews 13:2. Put
   down some of your thoughts about angels.

   c. Which verse did you choose to memorize this week? What was
   your reason for choosing this verse?

55

HUMAN FAILURE AND THE GOODNESS OF GOD

GENESIS 3

Study Notes

Adam and Eve were placed in the Garden of Eden. Everybody has been interested in knowing where this garden was located. The majority of scholars have placed it in the valley of the Tigris and Euphrates Rivers, which is still a beautiful spot. The tall date palms grow and provide the people who now live in their shade with almost every necessity of life. The fresh luscious dates are one of their chief foods. The garden provided richly for Adam and Eve as well. God gave man dominion over all things that God had created. Even the beasts of the field were obedient to the will of our first parents, Adam and Eve.

Man's Fall into Sin Genesis 3:1-7

The first temptation to do wrong came through a serpent. All through the Bible "serpent" is the word used for Satan or the devil. The serpent was the most subtle or wisest of all animal creation (2 Corinthians 11:3; Revelation 12:9; 20:2). The serpent was also the most beautiful creature, and the devil wanted to hide himself behind something that looked good. He wanted to use the best thing he could find. He almost always hides behind something good.

57

Someone has said that "good" is the worst enemy of "best." What does this mean? Yes, it means that often we are fooled into accepting the thing that is not too bad instead of accepting God's will which is best.

The devil is the master of deceit. "Satan, who is the god of this evil world, has made him blind, unable to see the glorious light of the Gospel that is shining upon him, or to understand the amazing message we preach about the glory of Christ, who is God" (2 Corinthians 4:4).

Yes, Satan does deceive. See 2 Corinthians 11:13,14; Ephesians 6:11,12; 2 Thessalonians 2:9.

The first temptation of Eve began with questioning what God had told her to do. The serpent asked a subtle question: "Has God said, 'You shall not eat from any tree of the garden'?" (Genesis 3:1).The serpent knew what God had said about this tree in Genesis 2:16,17: "From any tree of the garden you may eat freely; but from the tree of the knowledge of good and evil you shall not eat, for in the day that you eat from it you shall surely die."

Notice that one step led to the next. First there was a lingering look; second, a yearning desire; third, a willing action. This sin began with the eye, then used the mouth, next engaged the mind, then involved the hand.

In Eve's reply to the serpent she added to the Word of God—a very dangerous practice. She said that they could not eat nor "touch" the tree lest they die. This can serve as a warning to us today. We are not to add to the Scriptures, God's Word, or to remove anything from God's Word.

Proverbs 30:5,6 tells us "Every word of God is flawless; he is a shield to those who take refuge in him. Do not add to his words, or he will rebuke you and prove you a liar." "Do everything that I have commanded you; do not add anything to it or take anything from it" (Deuteronomy 12:32).

Do you receive all of God's Word as His truth? Have you ever considered adding to it some of men's writing? Have you ever taken away parts of His written Word because you didn't want to agree with it? Psalm 119:89: "For ever, O Lord, thy word is settled in heaven." *Let us never be guilty of adding to or taking away from the Word of God which the Holy Spirit led men to record for us and which is settled in heaven for all eternity.*

The serpent put into Eve's heart the wicked thought that some

58

other plan than God's plan was best. Does Satan ever do that now? Yes indeed! *The best time to overcome such a temptation is the minute it is first suggested.* Don't give yourself time to think it over! "Neither give place to the devil" (Ephesians 4:27). Don't give him an opportunity to tempt you. "Resist the devil, and he will flee from you" (James 4:7). Jesus Christ has delivered us from the power of Satan and translated us into the Kingdom of God because of our faith in Him (Colossians 1:13). Always remember that "greater is he [Jesus Christ] that is in you, than he [Satan] that is in the world" (1 John 4:4).

The temptation which Eve experienced was not sin. It was the yielding to temptation which became the sin in Adam and Eve's life. And since that time we discover from reading our Bible that "all have sinned, and come short of the glory of God" (Romans 3:23). However, our loving heavenly Father has provided forgiveness for this sin—"For the wages of sin is death; but the gift of God is eternal life through Jesus Christ our Lord" (Romans 6:23).

There is constant warfare between good and evil, between God's plan for us and Satan's design upon us. There is no end to the fight on earth, the beginning of which we study in Genesis 3. God has promised that whatever the temptation, there is also a way out.

"But remember this—the wrong desires that come into your life aren't anything new and different. Many others have faced exactly the same problems before you. And no temptation is irresistible. You can trust God to keep the temptation from becoming so strong that you can't stand up against it, for he has promised this and will do what he says. He will show you how to escape temptation's power so that you can bear up patiently against it" (1 Corinthians 10:13).

God has also given us His Word which He expects us to use in times of temptation. In Matthew 4:1-10 and Luke 4:1-13, we read of Satan's temptation of the Lord Jesus Christ. Jesus Christ answered each temptation of Satan with the phrase "it is written" and proceeded to quote Scripture to Satan.

We also have this same weapon available to us today. *Are you hiding the Word of God in your heart so that you will not sin against Him?* (Psalm 119:11). Are you using the Word of God to meet temptations and to give you victory in them? Are you saying to Satan, "Be gone," as Jesus Christ did in Matthew 4:10?

Jesus Christ has promised to give us victory. He has also given us guidelines in how He will provide that victory. Will you choose today to seek the Lord's help in any temptation which you know exists in your life?

Temptation often causes us to question God's goodness. Don't ever question God's love. You can always be sure that God does what is best for you. You may not always understand, but you can always be sure that God's care is so great that He can keep you from falling. We can't see the future as God can, but one day we will be able to look back and know that God has acted in love in every area of our lives as we have trusted Him.

First a question and then a lie; that is the way the devil works. In Genesis 3:4,5 the serpent said to the woman, "You will not surely die. For God knows that in the day you eat of it your eyes will be opened, and you will be like God, knowing good and evil." The tempter began with a mean, insinuating question about God's love and then a flat contradiction of what God said.

Eve doubted God. Her eyes looked; she saw. That was the beginning of it all. Then she argued with herself and reached out her hand.

Notice that one step led to the next. First there was a lingering look; second, a yearning desire; third, a willing action. This sin began with the eye, then used the mouth, next engaged the mind, then involved the hand.

Today, we too experience a sense of guilt from sin until we have asked the Lord Jesus Christ to forgive it. We may try to hide our guilt in the doing of good deeds, in the giving of money to worthy causes, and in performing other kindnesses. Yet these things cannot cover past sins. First John 1:9 gives us the answer to our guilt. We are to confess our sins and to ask forgiveness in the name of Jesus Christ.

We need to watch our eyes. The eye opens the door to most of the sin that is done. Eve's eyes opened the door to her appetite. .

In 1 John 2:16 we read, "For all that is in the world—the lust of the flesh, and the lust of the eyes, and the pride of life—is not of the Father, but is of the world." These three categories are the very ones that the devil used in the temptation of Eve. She sinned with her eyes, for in Genesis 3:6 we read that the fruit was pleasant to the eyes. She sinned with her mouth, or the lust of the flesh, for she saw that the "tree was good for food." She sinned with her hand when she took the fruit. She thought it would make her wise. This was the pride of life.

Does sin generally affect others beside the one doing the sinning? Yes! This is all too true. As surely as you sin, someone you love will suffer. Eve's hand did two things. It took the fruit and gave it to her

60

husband. Sin is so selfish! No person sins alone. If you take hold of a sooty, black stick, and then in turn take hold of someone else's hand, that person's hand will be blackened also. And so will everything else be that you touch. A better policy is to stop before you do the thing that is wrong.

Adam blamed Eve, and Eve blamed the serpent. Why do we blame others for our wrongdoing? Do you defend yourself when you sin? It is so easy to give an excuse for what you do instead of confessing that the act is sin, and asking God to forgive you (1 John 1:9). Learn not to blame others for what you do. Face the truth. God already knows about it; you can't fool Him!

What is the penalty for sin? Death! "But the gift of God is eternal life through Jesus Christ our Lord" (Romans 6:23). Have you received "eternal life," a gift from God, through Jesus Christ?

God said in Genesis 2:17 that if Adam and Eve ate of the fruit of the tree, they would surely die. *Our life is from God. Whatever separates us from Him cuts us off from life.* If you cut a branch off a tree, the branch is dead because it has been separated from its source of life. It may not look dead immediately, but just wait a few days. ?

In the same chapter that records this story of sin is the promise of victory over it. God is never late. Read Genesis 3:15, for here a Redeemer is promised! (This promise will be discussed in the next section of the notes.) Adam and Eve were created as innocent persons with the power of choice. They could choose to break God's law if they wanted to. How sad it is that they wanted to. But then, don't you and I also break God's law? Or to be more correct, aren't you and I broken by God's law? *God did not make puppets of men. He gave each one of us a free will.*

The sin of Adam and Eve was an act of their own determination. The temptation came from the outside. *The first sin was very much like every sin which has been committed. The sin was disbelief in the Word of the Living God, a belief in Satan rather than a belief in God.*

The same kinds of temptation that came to Adam and Eve came to Christ in the wilderness, and the same kinds have come to men ever since (1 John 2:15-17). First, the devil came to Christ with the temptation that He turn the stones into bread. Certainly, this was an attempt to make Christ sin by yielding to the lust of the flesh. Second, the devil told the Lord Jesus Christ to cast Himself down from the pinnacle of the temple. Here was a temptation to yield to the sin of pride of life. Third, the devil showed the Lord all the kingdoms of the world. What an example of a sin to yield to the lust of the eye. The devil makes great offers; so great, he even dared to make them to Christ (Matthew 4:1-11).

All men since the Fall, without respect to position or class, have

61

been sinners before God. "There is none righteous, no, not one" (Romans 3:10). "Wherefore, as by one man sin entered into the world, and death by sin; and so death passed upon all men, for that all have sinned" (Romans 5:12). The entire nature of man has been brought under the condemnation and curse.

1. His understanding is darkened (Ephesians 4:18).
2. His heart is deceitful (Jeremiah 17:9).
3. The mind and conscience are defiled (Titus 1:15).
4. The flesh is defiled (Galatians 5:17).
5. The will is weakened (Romans 7:18).
6. We are destitute of any qualities which meet the requirement of God's holiness (Romans 7:18).

The Judgment of God upon the Sin
Genesis 3:8-13

The first result of Adam and Eve's sin was that their eyes were opened "and they knew that they were naked" (Genesis 3:7). They knew they were uncovered before God. So they took fig leaves and sewed them together to make themselves aprons. Then they hid from God because their guilt made them ashamed before God (Genesis 3:8).

Today, we too experience a sense of guilt from sin until we have asked the Lord Jesus Christ to forgive it. We may try to hide our guilt in the doing of good deeds, in the giving of money to worthy causes, and in performing other kindnesses. Yet these things cannot cover past sins. First John 1:9 gives us the answer to our guilt. We are to confess our sins and to ask forgiveness in the name of Jesus Christ.

The Bible tells us whatever is not of faith is sin (Romans 14:23). However, when we bring our sin to God and ask Him to forgive us, because of our faith in Jesus Christ our sins are covered and forgiven. We need not feel guilty about them anymore. "Though your sins be as scarlet, they shall be as white as snow" (Isaiah 1:18).

We find that Adam and Eve were actually playing a game of hide-and-seek in the Garden of Eden. These were two people who were trying to prevent God from finding them. Before this Adam and God had sweet fellowship, but now all that had disappeared. And the reason was sin.

Adam tried to conceal his whereabouts from God also, because he misunderstood the Lord entirely. He forgot that the Lord was seeking him in order to clothe and save him. For God surely knew that Adam and Eve had sinned before He actually saw them face-to-face in the garden. *God loved them and wanted to save them.*

Once a little boy wandered into the woods and was lost for two hours. Finally, he found his way home, but fearing his father's anger because he was so late, he decided to hide in a barn until morning. His parents loved him so much that they spent the whole night searching for him through the fields, in the marsh, and in the woods. If he had only known of their heartfelt concern, he would not have needed to spend hours of fear, cold, and discomfort in a barn instead of in his soft bed. Yes, God loves you, too! He is waiting for you to run to Him just as the parents of the lost child desired him to run to them. Have you ever in faith run to the Lord Jesus Christ?

God's Punishment Comes with Promise
Genesis 3:14-19

The serpent was condemned by God and a curse was put upon him. "Cursed are you more than all cattle, and more than every beast of the field; on your belly shall you go, and dust shall you eat all the days of your life" (Genesis 3:14). In Genesis 3:15, the punishment passes beyond the reptile to the devil himself. As the Bible says, "I will put enmity between you and the woman, and between your seed and her seed; He shall bruise you on the head, and you shall bruise him on the heel." The seed of "the woman" mentioned here is the first promise in the Bible of Christ, who would be born of a virgin (Isaiah 7:14; Luke 1:34,35).

The entire Bible is occupied with the development and fulfillment of this promise of a coming Savior. Christ was to be born of a virgin and He was coming to put an end to the work of the devil by His death and resurrection. The phrase "bruise his heel" refers to Christ's suffering when He was "bruised for our iniquities" (Isaiah 53:5).

In the other half of this prophecy we are told that the woman's seed "shall bruise thy head" which speaks of the devil. This refers to the victory of the Cross and the resurrection of our Lord Jesus Christ. "Since we, God's children, are human beings—made of flesh and blood—he became flesh and blood too by being born in human form; for only as a human being could he die and in dying break the power of the devil who had the power of death" (Hebrews 2:14).

Adam and Eve also received punishment. Eve would have multiplied pain in childbearing and dependence upon her husband as he ruled over her. Adam was to have multiplied work. His former delightful work of keeping the garden was now to become a toil on land which brought forth thistles and thorns. He would begin to suffer all of the tensions and anxieties which breadwinners today experience. Genesis 3:19 also tells us that death would become the sorrow of the human race. Satan said they would not die if they ate of the

63

fruit, yet Adam and all of his descendants died.

The Goodness of God's Goodness Toward Adam and Eve Genesis 3:20-24

Adam and Eve were ashamed because of their sin. They tried to cover themselves by making clothes out of fig leaves, but this did not satisfy God. He wanted to teach them an important lesson. He wanted them to know that "without shedding of blood is no remission" of sin (Hebrews 9:22). To teach this lesson God made them clothing from the skins of animals. Of course, the animals had to be killed in order that Adam and Eve could get the skins. So you see, the blood of animals was shed (Genesis 3:21).

How wonderful God is! Sin must be punished, but God has a way by which we may be forgiven. God told Adam and Eve His plan in Genesis 3:15. The seed of the woman is to be Jesus Christ, our Redeemer.

From that time forth every woman hoped her child would be the promised Deliverer. This is one reason why the genealogies (family records) were recorded so carefully for us in the Bible. They proved the direct human genealogy of the Lord Jesus Christ back to Adam (Luke 3:23-38). So you see, when Adam and Eve sinned, God already had a plan by which their sin could be forgiven. This promise (Genesis 3:15) shows us that Jesus Christ is the Savior and when we accept Him to be our very own Savior, He forgives our sins.

Just as God loved Adam and Eve and promised that some day a Savior would come, so He loves us and tells us that Christ is our Savior (John 3:16,17,36). God loved us so much that He gave His only Son. Look at these verses in John 3 and put your name in place of "the world." Make your choice today for Jesus Christ if you have never done it before.

You may wonder about those who lived during the Old Testament days, and how they could receive forgiveness for sins and eternal life. In the Old Testament, faith in the promises of God led to eternal life. The promises of God were to be fulfilled in Jesus Christ. Today, faith in the revealed Son of God and His death on the cross for our sins is the only way to eternal life. Read Hebrews 11, the great faith chapter, which mentions many of the Old Testament men and women.

We find that in Genesis 3:22 God removed Adam and Eve from the garden "lest he put forth his hand, and take also of the tree of life, and eat, and live forever." Adam was sent out to till the ground from which he was made. Then at the east of the Garden of Eden, God placed the cherubim and a flaming sword which turned every way, to guard the way to the Tree of Life.

The cherubim are actually heavenly beings mentioned in the Scriptures. Their likeness was to be embroidered upon the Holy Veil and carved upon the Ark (Exodus 25:18-22; 26:1). God was symbolically described as riding upon a cherub in Psalm 18:10. The apostle John described seeing these same cherubim in Revelation 4:6-9; 5:6-14; 6:1-8. We do not know if the description is intended to be symbolic or an actual fact, but we do know that the Bible portrays them as "living beings." They appear as a winged animal with faces of lion, ox, man or eagle.

The way back into the Garden of Eden was also guarded by a revolving sword-like flame. Fire is used throughout the Bible to symbolize the holiness of God. Hebrews 12:29 says "our God is a consuming fire." God revealed Himself to Moses in a burning bush (Exodus 3:2). God burned and cleansed the "unclean" lips of Isaiah with fire (Isaiah 6:5-7).

God was greatly grieved at the sin of Adam and Eve. He knew that all suffering, sickness and death would be the result of this sin. God still loved Adam and Eve but He could not excuse their sin even if it seemed like such a little thing to them.

Here is a story which illustrates the power of a little sin: There existed an old elm tree which was 100 feet tall and four feet in diameter. It was a giant tree which stood by a home for many years. People had admired its stately branches for decades. They had been impressed by its strength and endurance. Perhaps two hundred or three hundred years old, it had weathered many a storm. It withstood a tornado. Once it was struck by a bolt of lightning, and many times its branches hung almost to the ground under the weight of ice from a sleet storm. However, it recovered after each test and kept on growing.

Then suddenly it grew sick and its leaves fell off weeks before their time. The mighty elm died. The proud, powerful giant fell before the attack of an almost invisible fungus carried by a tiny insect—the Dutch Elm beetle. What wind and storm and lightning could not do, a tiny bug had succeeded in doing.

Surely this is the picture of many Christians' downfall. It is the story of fatal "little sins." Many a person has withstood great trials and severe temptations, only to fail before some so-called "little sin" of greed, pride, or envy. The sin of Adam did not seem serious—just taking a piece of fruit from a forbidden tree—but it resulted in death for himself, for his offspring, and for all creation of which he was the head.

Today watch for the little temptations—and the big ones will be easier to meet. It is "the little foxes that spoil the vines" (Song of Solomon 2:15). "Resist the devil, and he will flee from you" (James 4:7).

"For God is at work within you, helping you want to obey him, and then helping you do what he wants" (Philippians 2:13). "For I can do everything God asks me to with the help of Christ who gives me the strength and power" (Philippians 4:13).

Will you trust God this week to give you His strength and power for all of your needs and for all that He asks you to do by Jesus Christ's strength?

Study Questions

Before you begin your study this week:
1. Pray and ask God to speak to you through His Holy Spirit each day.
2. Use only your Bible for your answers.
3. Write your answers and the verses you have used.
4. Challenge questions are for those who have the time and wish to do them.
5. Personal questions are to be shared with your study group only if you wish to share.
6. As you study look for a verse to memorize this week. Write it down, carry it with you, tack it to your bulletin board, tape it to the dashboard of your car. Make a real effort to learn the verse and its reference.

FIRST DAY: Read the notes and the Scripture references given in the notes.

1. What was a helpful or new thought from the overview of Genesis 3?

2. What personal application did you select to apply to your own life this week?

SECOND DAY: Read all of Genesis 4, concentrating on verses 1-5.

1. What name and occupation did the two sons of Adam and Eve have?

2 a. In time God asked both Cain and Abel for a sacrifice. What did each of them give to God?

b. How did the Lord react to these offerings?

67

3. **Challenge:** Read Hebrews 11:4. Why do you believe that God received Abel's sacrifice as more excellent than Cain's?

4. Apparently both Cain and Abel had been told of the necessity of a blood sacrifice as an expression of their faith in God to forgive their sins. This offering was to be the beginning of the picture the Old Testament paints for us to point toward the coming of the Messiah, Jesus Christ. What do the following verses say about Jesus Christ?

   John 1:29

   Mark 14:24

   Acts 20:28

   Ephesians 5:2

5. Cain offered only the fruit of his own labor in the field. God never did and never will accept our own works as a means of forgiveness of sin. Share in your own words what the following verses tell you about your own "good works."

   Isaiah 57:12

   Romans 3:20

Ephesians 2:8,9

2 Timothy 1:9

6 a. What are some "good works" which people today "hand to God" instead of trusting His Son to forgive them their sins?

b. (Personal) Look at your own life. Have you been trying to earn God's favor by the fruit of your own toil just as Cain did? Only through faith in the Lamb of God, the Lord Jesus Christ, can we please God and be accepted and forgiven by Him. Have you ever invited Christ into your life?

THIRD DAY: Read Genesis 4:5-7.

1. What was Cain's response to God's disregard of his offering?

2 a. Read the following verses to discover what the Bible says about man's anger. Put them in your own words.

Psalm 37:8

Proverbs 14:17

Proverbs 16:32

James 1:19

b. (Personal) Which of the above suggestions concerning anger would you like to ask Jesus Christ to help you with today? How does Philippians 4:13 encourage you concerning control of anger?

3. Read Galatians 5:19-21. Find in these verses the emotions you think Cain probably had toward his brother at this time.

4. **Challenge:** Do you believe that God was giving Cain another opportunity to give the proper sacrifice, according to what He said in Genesis 4:7?

5 a. What does God tell Cain to conquer in Genesis 4:7?

b. What do the following verses promise you when you are tempted to sin?

James 4:7

James 1:12

1 Corinthians 10:13

c. Do you believe that we should teach our youth the above promises from the Bible? Give your reasons for your answer.

70

6 a. Do you see God's tender love for Cain as He gives him opportunity to obey by giving a blood sacrifice to Him? What is God's question to Cain which shows His deep love and concern for him?

   b. (Personal) Do you sense God's tender love toward you today? Do you have an unhappy heart? God wants to help you. See Psalm 31:19.

FOURTH DAY: Read Genesis 4:8-10.

1. What sin did Cain not resist according to Genesis 4:8?

2 a. According to Matthew 9:4, where does temptation first strike us?

   b. Do you believe that Cain entertained the thought of killing his brother before he actually did the deed?

   c. Who do we need to give our "thought life" to?

3. What does Romans 12:1,2 say that the Christian should do? Who will "renew our mind"?

4 a. What two questions did God ask Cain?

   b. Do you believe that God knew what Cain had done to Abel? What statement does God make which makes you believe this? Give verse.

71

5. Do you believe that God sees our sins? What do the following verses say concerning this?

Jeremiah 2:22

Jeremiah 16:17

Psalm 90:8

Psalm 94:11

6 a. What does God promise that He will do if we confess our sin to Him? See 1 John 1:9.

b. (Personal) Have you done what 1 John 1:9 instructs you to do today? Why not stop and talk to God right now about this?

FIFTH DAY: Read Genesis 4:11-16.

1 a. What was the result of Cain's sin according to Genesis 4:11,12?

b. From whose face would Cain be "hid" or kept from because of his sin? Do you believe this saddened God's loving heart?

2. What did Cain fear?

3. What did God say concerning Cain's fear and what did He do about it in Genesis 4:15?

4. Where did Cain go to live, and whose presence did he no longer have the pleasure of?

5 a. Do you believe that it was Cain's deliberate choice which caused this separation from God?

   b. **Challenge:** What choice do people deliberately make today which separates them from God? See John 14:6 to help you with your answer.

6 a. In what ways do you think you could help someone who has done this today?

   b. What does Joshua 24:15 say about choice?

   c. (Personal) Would you like to choose to use any part of Joshua 24:15 in your life today? Share with your discussion group if possible.

SIXTH DAY: Read Genesis 4:17-26.

1. What did Cain name the city he built? Why did he call it this?

2. God had planned for each man to have only one wife. Who was the first descendant of Cain to practice polygamy?

3. What were some of the things Cain's descendants began to develop? Give verses.

4. What sin did Lamech brag about according to Genesis 4:23?

5. What was the name of the third son that Adam and Eve had?

6 a. What good thing did Seth and his sons do?

   b. What does God promise if we call on His name? See Psalm 91:15,16.

   c. What Scripture verse did you choose to memorize this week?

UNBELIEF DESTROYS; TRUST IN GOD DELIVERS

GENESIS 4

Study Notes

How different the world became as a result of Adam and Eve's sin, "The Fall." Animals became ferocious and men were fearful of them. Thorns and thistles grew. Men became giants upon the earth. The civilization that Adam and Eve tried to set up was doomed from the very beginning because sin was at work in it. We see man's selfishness bearing its deadly fruit. *All sin has its roots in and grows up out of unbelief. Man became self-centered instead of God-centered. Self is the heart of all sin.*

God is the center of true life. Remember, a phonograph record with the hole a little off center makes a terrible noise. Instead of beautiful music there is nothing but discord! But put the phonograph record back on the center, and the discord turns into lovely music. The record has not been changed at all. The difference is all in the "center"!

God wants our lives to be a beautiful symphony of music. Everything that He creates and plans is beautiful. He plans our lives with Himself as center. If we have self as the center, we find that our days are full of confusion and unhappiness.

We will see from Genesis 4 that Cain put self at the center of his life. Cain's sin separated him from his brother and shows us how, sin separates men and women from their brothers and sisters. Remember, sin separates you from God and separates you from your fellow men.

75

If we do what 1 John 1:9 tells us to do, we need no longer be separated from God by our sin. "If we say that we have no sin, we deceive ourselves, and the truth is not in us. If we confess our sins, he is faithful and just to forgive us our sins, and to cleanse us from all unrighteousness" (1 John 1:8,9). We need to use this principle from God's Word each day and keep "short accounts" with God. Have you talked to the Lord today?

Adam and Eve's Two Children, Cain and Abel Genesis 4:1-2

In Genesis 4:1 we find that Adam and Eve had their first child, Cain. The Hebrew meaning of Cain is "acquisition." Eve had heard the promise concerning the seed of the woman (Genesis 3:15) and had believed that her child would be the answer to this promise from God. She may have even believed that they would soon be back in Eden.

Each of us has to make the choice! Will we obey self and its desires, or will we do what God says? If you are allowing your attitude to be controlled by yourself rather than by God, you need to recognize this as a sin against God and take responsibility for it. The wonderful thing is that you can receive God's cleansing and complete deliverance from this rebellion through Jesus Christ's forgiveness. Recognize that He loves you and thank Him for this love.

So she named the baby "here it is"! For that is the meaning of Cain. But the baby turned out to be the first murderer, not the promised deliverer from sin. The promise in Genesis 3:15 refers to the Messiah, the Lord Jesus Christ, who would come in God's time to deliver man from the sin that was brought into the world by Adam and Eve.

"Wherefore, as by one man sin entered into the world, and death by sin; and so death passed upon all men, for that all have sinned" (Romans 5:12). "For as by one man's disobedience [Adam] many were made sinners; so by the obedience of one [the Lord Jesus Christ] shall many be made righteous" (Romans 5:19).

Yes, sin entered the world when Adam and Eve sinned, but God in Genesis 3:15 promised a Redeemer who would provide forgiveness for sin and open the way for us to come to God. The Bible tells us

"For the wages of sin is death; but the gift of God is eternal life through Jesus Christ our Lord" (Romans 6:23). Have you recognized the wonderful free gift that God provided for you in Jesus Christ our Lord? Are you sharing this wonderful gift with others?

After Eve gave birth to Cain she gave birth to a second son named Abel. The name means "that which ascends." No doubt Adam and Eve spent much time teaching their sons. They must have told them about the beautiful garden home where they had once lived.

I am sure that Adam and Eve told them about the importance of obeying God. They must have explained how God killed animals to give them skins for clothes (Genesis 3:21). Over and over again, these two parents probably told the boys that they must always do exactly as God told them to do.

Adam and Eve had learned the unhappy results of not doing what God had told them to do. It had been a bitter lesson for them. Remember, it was because they did not obey God that they were forced to leave the Garden of Eden. When each of the boys was old enough, he decided the way in which he would make his living. Cain became a farmer and plowed the ground and raised fruit and grain. Abel became a shepherd and spent his time raising sheep (Genesis 4:2).

Cain and Abel's Offerings and Attitudes Genesis 4:3-7

During their childhood Cain and Abel no doubt saw their father bring offerings to the Lord. Probably they had taken part in the family worship. Their worship took the form of offerings. In those days people built altars of stone upon which they laid their offerings. As Cain and Abel grew up, each of them brought an offering to the Lord.

The Bible says, "And Abel, he also brought of the firstlings of his flock and of the fat thereof. And the Lord had respect unto Abel and to his offering" (Genesis 4:4). God looked into Abel's heart and recognized his heart attitude was right toward Him.

But Cain brought some fruit or grain from the field. It was probably the very best fruit he had ever raised. Yet God looked into his heart and saw that he gave his offering with a wrong attitude, probably out of a sense of duty only.

It is true today that some people continue to take Cain's attitude and try to worship God out of sense of duty, rather than out of a heart of love for the Lord Jesus Christ. This worship is not acceptable to God today either.

What was Cain's offering worth in God's sight? Nothing, worse than nothing, because Cain made his offering in his own way. God was not pleased with his unbelief. "It was by faith that Abel obeyed God and brought an offering that pleased God more than Cain's offering did. God accepted Abel and proved it by accepting his gift; and though Abel is long dead, we can still learn lessons from him about trusting God" (Hebrews 11:4). The Bible says "unto Cain and to his offering he had not respect" (Genesis 4:5).

God never did and never will accept our own works as a means of forgiveness of sin. Nothing we do can make us clean in the sight of God. The Bible tells us that all of our righteousness, or good works, are as "filthy rags" in God's eyes (Isaiah 64:6).

Paul, writing to the Ephesians, makes it very clear that any works on our part cannot save us. "For by grace [God's Riches at Christ's Expense] are ye saved through faith; and that not of yourselves: it is the gift of God: not of works, lest any man should boast" (Ephesians

By the Holy Spirit, God reveals to us today whether or not our life and works are accepted by Him. Just as a medical doctor must diagnose our illnesses in order to give us medicine to heal us, so God, by the Holy Spirit, points out our sin and then provides healing through the Lord Jesus Christ.

2:8,9). "So also Christ died only once as an offering for the sins of many people" (Hebrews 9:28). Have you opened your heart in real love to the Lord Jesus Christ?

We find that Cain is called the wicked one in 1 John 3:12. His life is condemned in Jude 1:11, and his works are called evil in 1 John 3:12. The reason he is described this way is because he did not believe God and made his offering only out of a sense of duty.

Abel is called righteous in Hebrews 11:4. His works are called righteous in 1 John 3:12, and Jesus Christ called him righteous in Matthew 23:35. Hebrews 11:4 tells us that Abel sacrificed because he had faith in God.

Both Cain and Abel showed what their hearts were like when they offered to God their sacrifices. *God knew* their hearts and God knows our hearts today, for "The Lord seeth not as a man seeth; for man looketh on the outward appearance, but the Lord looketh on·the heart" (1 Samuel 16:7). How is it with your heart attitude today? Could God describe you by the terms He used for Cain in the Scriptures? Or would God describe you by the terms used for Abel in the Scriptures?

Each of us has to make the choice! Will we obey self and its desires, or will we do what God says? If you are allowing your attitude to be controlled by yourself rather than by God, you need to recognize this as a sin against God and take responsibility for it. The wonderful thing is that you can receive God's cleansing and complete deliverance from this rebellion through Jesus Christ's forgiveness. Recognize that He loves you and thank Him for this love.

When the Lord was here on earth many years later, He was introduced as the Lamb of God. "Behold the Lamb of God, which taketh away the sin of the world" (John 1:29). Abel brought a lamb for sacrifice and this lamb was a picture of the Lord Jesus who would some day come and be the perfect sacrifice for our sins.

The blood sacrifice of the Old Testament was also a visual aid from God, that He would one day send the Messiah, Jesus Christ, to die on the cross and shed His blood for us to give us salvation. We are saved from sin by this precious blood of Jesus Christ, the Lamb of God. We are brought back to God from sin as we acknowledge Jesus Christ and invite Him into our lives as our Savior and Lord. "For as much as ye know that ye were not redeemed with corruptible things, as silver and gold . . . but with the precious blood of Christ, as of a lamb without blemish and without spot" (1 Peter 1:18,19).

We do not have to offer a sacrifice now. Christ is our sacrifice. Yet today people are still offering good works instead of trusting the Lord Jesus Christ to forgive them their sins.

What are you depending upon today—good works or Jesus Christ? Are you trying to earn God's favor by dutifully doing good works just as Cain did? Or have you been obedient to God as Abel was by believing on the Lord Jesus Christ?

Although God did not accept Cain's sacrifice, He had loving compassion on him as He recognized his angry feelings and unhappiness and hurt. God saw in Cain's face this unhappiness and came to him in his hour of need (Genesis 4:7). He was willing to give him a chance to be free of his resentment and jealousy of Abel before it reached the place of no return. The love of God had provided what was necessary for bringing the sinner to Himself, the sin offering which Abel had already given.

In Genesis 4:7 we find the Hebrew word *chattath* which is translated "sin." It is frequently found translated "sin offering." Thus God was saying to Cain in effect, "If your conscience accuses you of sin, there is a sin offering crouching or waiting for you outside of your door." God was telling Cain that His standard for forgiveness of sins still stood, but He was offering Cain a way of escape. *He wanted Cain to take the way of escape by offering the sin offering so that he would be accepted by God and could be loved as Abel was loved.*

79

By the Holy Spirit, God reveals to us today whether or not our life and works are accepted by Him. Just as a medical doctor must diagnose our illnesses in order to give us medicine to heal us, so God, by the Holy Spirit, points out our sin and then provides healing through the Lord Jesus Christ. The Holy Spirit also helps us to know that, when we receive Jesus Christ as our Savior and Lord, we have been accepted by God and are forgiven and loved by Him. "The Spirit itself beareth witness with our spirit, that we are the children of God" (Romans 8:16). *Thus we see that God does accept Christ's sacrifice for our sin and the Holy Spirit makes this real to us.*

If you have invited Jesus Christ into your life as your Savior and Lord, He has put His seal upon you by the presence of the Holy Spirit in your life (Ephesians 1:13). Do you have the Holy Spirit as the seal of God's acceptance in your life?

Cain Slays Abel Genesis 4:8-16

When Cain saw that his offering was not accepted, he was very angry. Certainly God was displeased by what Cain had done and at the anger that Cain felt for Abel. Soon anger turned to hate and then hate to murder. Cain killed his own brother!

All of us are susceptible to anger. One man accused of losing his temper, burst out, "But I never lost my temper once if I got what I wanted." *The old nature becomes angriest when it is crossed. Wanting one's own way is the worst sin because it is the first of sins. It leads to all others.*

Proverbs 14:17 says, "A quick-tempered man acts foolishly." As Christians we are instructed to be swift to hear, slow to speak, and slow to anger in James 1:19. Only as we rely upon the Lord Jesus Christ and His strength can we hope to have God's help in conquering anger in our lives before it leads to greater sin (Philippians 4:13).

Cain would not listen to the Lord. Cain entertained the thought of killing his brother before he actually did the deed. Often our temptation begins in our thought life, too. The Bible promises, "No temptation has overtaken you but such as is common to man; and God is faithful, who will not allow you to be tempted beyond what you are able, but with the temptation will provide the way of escape also, that you may be able to endure it" (1 Corinthians 10:13).

God had offered Cain a way of escape in Genesis 4:7, but Cain continued to rebel against God. *God always provides a way out of our temptation, too. We must make our choice of whether to receive God's help or not.*

Cain thought no one saw him kill his brother. But who always sees what we do? (Jeremiah 2:22; 16:17; Psalm 90:8; 94:11). "The Lord said unto Cain, Where is Abel thy brother?" (Genesis 4:9).

Now Cain added one more sin to his list. One sin always leads to another. First, he was angry. Second, he killed his brother. And third, Cain told a lie. He lied to God! He said, "I know not: Am I my brother's keeper?" (Genesis 4:9).

Cain was required by God in Genesis 4:9 to give an account of his deeds. The Bible tells us that both the Christian and the non-Christian will be judged and will have to give an account to God one day. The Christian will stand before the judgment seat of Christ (Romans 14:10; 2 Corinthians 5:10). The last judgment is recorded in Revelation 20:11-15, and here the doom of those who have never received the Lord Jesus Christ by faith is foretold.

Cain's reply to God, "Am I my brother's keeper?" suggests that Cain felt God should be taking care of His own world and shouldn't be bothering him with questions about His creatures. Cain must have believed that God would not see his sin! He had forgotten God's perfect wisdom! God punished Cain for his sin, for sin must always be punished. Cain had deliberately rejected God's offered way of escape in Genesis 4:7.

Genesis 4:12 tells us what Cain's punishment was. He would work the ground and it would yield less than the strength it had. He would also become a fugitive, a vagabond, who would wander across the earth. Is it any wonder that Cain said, "My punishment is greater than I can bear"?

In Genesis 4:14 we read that his punishment would also be that he would be hid from the face of God. The separation from God would bring fear in Cain's heart and would cause him to believe that everyone would seek to slay him. There wasn't a hint of sorrow in Cain's words to God concerning his punishment, and no hint of repentance.

Surely God must have pitied Cain as he fled from Him. Cain's loss is eternal. God allowed him to keep his earthly life, but he lived away from the presence of God. Even the land he chose to dwell in, "Nod," means "wandering" (Genesis 4:16). In Genesis 4:15 the Lord set a mark upon Cain which can be considered a brand or a sign or a pledge.

Cain's Children: Sin, Then Silence
Genesis 4:17-24

The question is often asked, Where did Cain get his wife? By this time Adam and Eve had many sons and daughters and even grandchildren. Some believe that Adam and Eve's offspring could have numbered as many as thirty-two thousand by this time in Cain's life, for Adam was possibly one hundred and twenty-nine years old when Cain murdered Abel. These children of Adam would be the ones whom

Cain had feared might kill him in vengeance because he had killed their brother, Abel.

There was no law against a man marrying his near relatives at this time, and Cain, of course, married one of his sisters. The human race sprang from a single couple, Adam and Eve, so obviously they would have to marry close relatives in the early days. Adam married even closer than a sister; he married his own rib! The blood stream of man was fairly pure and there was no harm in close relatives marrying and having children in that day. The stream is always pure at the source. Every generation, like the cities on the bank of a stream, puts its sewage into the human race.

In Genesis 4:17 we learn that Cain built a city and called it after the name of his first son, Enoch. This name Enoch meant "dedication." People today can appear to be dedicated in certain ways. Yet God looks upon their hearts and knows what is in their hearts, just as He looked upon Cain's heart and knew his heart. *He called his son "dedication" but he had never given himself up to God.*

Do you call yourself dedicated to the Christian cause? Have you ever then given yourself up to God by trusting in His Son the Lord Jesus Christ? Have you given yourself up to God as a Christian?

"And so, dear brothers, I plead with you to give your bodies to God. Let them be a living sacrifice, holy—the kind he can accept. When you think of what he has done for you, is this too much to ask? Don't copy the behavior and customs of this world, but be a new and different person with a fresh newness in all you do and think. Then you learn from your own experience how His ways will really satisfy you" (Romans 12:1,2).

In Genesis 4:19 we find the beginning of polygamy on earth as Lamech takes two wives. The names of the woman are Adah "beauty" and Zillah "adornment." The meaning of these names indicates the values Lamech and his society were placing on womanhood. But God planned for woman to be a helpmate to her husband, not a showpiece (Genesis 3:16).

Many women in our society today put more emphasis on beauty and adornment than on seeking to be the godly women God planned for them to be. "Don't be concerned about the outward beauty that depends on jewelry, or beautiful clothes, or hair arrangement. Be beautiful inside, in your hearts, with the lasting charm of a gentle and quiet spirit which is so precious to God" (1 Peter 3:3,4).

The descendants of Cain went out from the presence of the Lord and thought they could make the world a happy place by building cities (Genesis 4:17), by developing agriculture (Genesis 4:20), by producing music and works of art (Genesis 4:21,22). Here is the attempt to make life easy, civilized, and safe. In Genesis 4:22 we read that Tubal-

Cain was an instructor of every artificer in brass and iron. Modern archeological excavations reveal the presence of city life at very early periods with evidences of the arts and crafts that are mentioned in Genesis 4:16-24.

The first murder by Cain was done in anger and envy, and the second murder was committed by Lamech in pride. Genesis 4:23,24 gives us the first recorded poetry of earth. "Listen to me, my wives. I have killed a youth that attacked and wounded me. If anyone who kills Cain will be punished seven times, anyone taking revenge against me for killing that youth, should be punished seventy-seven times!"

In this poem we find Lamech boasting of his bloody deed. The first murderer, Cain, has produced a descendant who became a murderer. After this picture of civilization and the triumphant poem of murder, there is only silence. We never hear of Cain's family again. In the space between Genesis 4:24 and Genesis 4:25 we begin to sense the rising of the waters of the flood in judgment against these people.

In Cain's civilization we see what has happened again and again in the history of the human race. Education, culture, and art are worshiped instead of God. These are God's own gifts to us, but are wrongly used by man. What is the main emphasis in your life today? Is it the cultural development of your present world? Does education, culture, and art take the place of God in your life? Or are you using these things properly as God's own gifts?

In what ways do you think you could help someone else who has made a wrong choice concerning these things? Have you prayed for that person yet today? Have you chosen to stand for God in your day? "Choose you this day whom ye will serve; . . . but as for me and my house, we will serve the Lord" (Joshua 24:15).

The Birth of Seth Assures the Savior's Line Genesis 4:25,26

Perhaps Satan thought that now he had spoiled God's promise of a Savior. Remember, God had promised Adam and Eve that someday He would send a Savior and this Savior would be born from one of the descendants of Adam and Eve (Genesis 3:15). Now Abel was dead and only Cain was left. But God had rejected Cain as one of the ancestors of His Son. God's plan would not be spoiled by the devil. Soon, another son, Seth, was born to Adam and Eve (Genesis 4:25). From the family of Seth, Christ would come.

The prophecy at the judgment of the serpent was that the seed of the woman would bruise the serpent's head. Satan immediately made war on God's plan and, in getting one son to kill his brother, the devil thought he had destroyed the possibility of God fulfilling the promise.

83

But God gave Adam and Eve another son whose name, Seth, means "appointed."

Seth had been appointed by God to replace Abel and to provide the line from which the seed would come. That seed would be the Lord Jesus Christ who would bruise the serpent's head, who could bring victory over Satan. This was to be the line of men who would respond to God.

In Genesis 4:26, we see that Seth had a son whom he called Enos and "then began men to call upon the name of the Lord." Seth and his sons put their trust in God. Have you put your trust in the Lord Jesus Christ?

"He shall call upon me, and I will answer him: I will be with him in trouble; I will deliver him, and honor him. With long life will I satisfy him, and show him my salvation" (Psalm 91:15,16). Have you put your trust in God and claimed these promises for yourself?

Study Questions

FIRST DAY: Read all of the notes and look up all of the Scriptures.

1. What was a helpful or new thought from the overview of Genesis 4?

2. What personal application did you select to apply to your own life this week?

SECOND DAY: Read Genesis 5.

1. How old was Adam when Seth was born?

2 a. What special fact do you learn about one of Adam's descendants? See Genesis 5:24.

b. (Personal) Would you like to have this said about you?

c. **Challenge:** What does the expression "walk with God" mean to you?

3. Of all of Adam's descendants listed here, who lived the longest?

4 a. What does Noah's name mean according to Genesis 5?

   b. (Personal) What part of the meaning of Noah's name would you
       like to be known by?

5 a. How do the following verses suggest ways in which you could
       "comfort" someone?

       Colossians 1:3

       Hebrews 10:24

       1 Thessalonians 2:11,12

       Acts 20:32

   b. (Personal) How could you be a comfort to your family, business
       associates, or friends this week?

6 a. According to Genesis 5, what did all of Adam's descendants
       (except for Enoch) do at the end of their lifetime?

b. Enoch "lived" because he walked with God. How can we "live" eternally?

John 6:27

John 5:24

THIRD DAY: Read 1 Thessalonians 4:16-18 with Genesis 5:24.

1. What happened to Enoch? Read Genesis 5:24.

2. Read the following Scriptures to find out more about Enoch.

Hebrews 11:5

Jude 1:14,15

3. Does God's removal of Enoch resemble the circumstances described in 1 Thessalonians 4:17,18?

4. According to 1 Thessalonians 4:17, who will the Christian meet in the air and how long will we be with Him?

5. Why did God plan for the Christian to know about this future thrilling event? See 1 Thessalonians 4:18.

6 a. What will be the signal to the Christians that these events are going to take place?

87

b. (Personal) What is the most exciting thought you have concerning 1 Thessalonians 4:16-18?

FOURTH DAY: Read Genesis 6, concentrating on verses 1-14.

1. Find the words which describe the human race at this time. Give verses.

2. What does this passage say about man's thoughts on sin in this day? Give verse.

3 a. According to Genesis 6:6, what were God's emotions concerning sinful man?

b. What did God decide to do about the sinfulness of man at this time?

c. What suffered because of man's sin according to Genesis 6:7?

4 a. How long did God plan to wait before he brought judgment on man's sin? See Genesis 6:3.

b. **Challenge:** Why do you believe that God was willing to wait this long? See 2 Peter 3:9 to help you with your answer.

5 a. How is Noah described in Genesis 6:9?

b. What did God instruct Noah to do? Give verse.

6 a. (Personal) Do you daily walk in fellowship with God and let God speak to you as Noah did?

b. What do the following verses say God will do for the Christian who walks in fellowship with Him?

Isaiah 57:15

2 Corinthians 6:16

John 14:23

c. (Personal) Which of the above promises from God means the most to you?

FIFTH DAY: Read Genesis 6:14-22.

1. Describe the ark from this passage. Give verses.

2. What would be killed by the flood according to Genesis 6:17?

3 a. Who was to go into the ark with Noah?

b. How many sons did Noah have and what were their names?

4. What else was Noah to take on the ark according to Genesis 6:19,20?

5. How was Noah to prepare for the journey on the ark according to Genesis 6:21?

6 a. Was Noah obedient to God?

b. The Bible teaches that if we love God we will obey Him also. What do the following verses say concerning this? Put them in your own words.

Ephesians 6:6

Hebrews 13:16

Hebrews 5:8,9

SIXTH DAY: Jesus Christ is the Christian's "Ark of Safety."

1. There was only one place of safety for Noah, and that was in the ark. There is only one place of safety for us and that is in the Lord Jesus Christ. Put the following verses into your own words concerning this fact.

John 10:9

1 John 5:11-13

John 3:16,17

Revelation 3:20

2. (Personal) Have you entered into a safe place by trusting in the Lord Jesus Christ as your Savior and Lord?

3. How could you help someone to know of the "safety" to be found in the Lord Jesus Christ? Think about the different ways you could help a child, an adolescent, and an adult to know Jesus Christ personally. Share your thoughts with your discussion group if possible.

4. **Challenge:** What do the following verses tell you about the Lord Jesus Christ?

Acts 4:12

John 14:6

Hebrews 11:6

5. How does Hebrews 11:7 describe Noah?

6. Which Scripture verse did you choose to memorize from the lesson this week? Why did you choose this verse?

MAN'S DISOBEDIENCE AND DESTRUCTION; GOD'S JUDGMENT AND LOVE

GENESIS 5-6

Study Notes

In Genesis 4 we discovered how Cain's descendants rejected God just as their father, Cain, had done (Genesis 4:16). In Genesis 4:25 God gave Adam and Eve another son, Seth. As we study Genesis 5 we will find that "men [Seth's sons] began to call upon the name of the Lord" (Genesis 4:26).

In Genesis 4 we find a humanistic culture which developed because Cain and his descendants had turned away from God. We see this same emphasis today because men are without God. Ours is a culture centered on man and those who follow it have no love for God.

The Godly Line: Adam to Jared
Genesis 5:1-17

In Genesis 5 we read of the development of a godly line which knew the Lord. They were known as followers of the Lord just as today

93

those who follow Christ are known as Christians. The first thing a person must do to follow the Lord is step out from the line of Cain into the line of Abel, carried on by Seth's descendants.

Hebrews 12:24 tells us that we are to come "to Jesus the mediator of the new covenant, and to the blood of sprinkling, that speaketh better things than that of Abel." God heard Abel's blood calling out in Genesis 4:10 against the first murder. Christ's blood is the solution to sin. The blood of Jesus Christ goes beyond justice and offers us God's mercy. "Christ also suffered. He died once for the sins of all us guilty sinners, although he himself was innocent of any sin at any time, that he might bring us safely home to God. But though his body died, his spirit lived on" (1 Peter 3:18).

When we receive Jesus Christ into our lives as our Savior and Lord, He brings us to God. We must recognize that we have gone astray, and ask Christ to bring us to God. *"All we like sheep have gone astray; we have turned every one to his own way"* (Isaiah 53:6). We cannot stand and point our finger at Cain or his descendants and deny

Enoch's walk with God was not a casual stroll. His walking with God implies that he had surrendered his will to God. He wanted to walk according to God's plan for his life. To walk with God is not an honor peculiar to Enoch; it is open to any one of us who has received Christ. It means that we are conscious of God's presence at all times.

that we, too, have gone astray. We must recognize our need to be brought into the presence of God by the Lord Jesus Christ. After we have asked Jesus Christ to take us to God we can go out and call others into God's presence with us.

God's wonderful promise and plan had existed before the beginning of time. "For since by man came death, by man came also the resurrection of the dead. For as in Adam all die, even so in Christ shall all be made alive" (1 Corinthians 15:21,22). *First Peter 1:20 emphasizes that it was the sacrificial death of Jesus which was "foreordained before the foundation of the world" by God. In Titus 1:2 we read that God promised eternal life "before the world began."*

Seth's name means "appointed," and his descendants were the line which called upon God in faith and obedience. To do so must have been an active choice on their part, since they lived in the world where Cain's descendants were also living. They could see how "the

94

other half" were living and therefore they made a deliberate choice to live differently in obedience to God.

The wasted years without God (Genesis 4) in Cain's line were not recorded, as they were of no value. *Yet the worthwhile years in Seth's line were documented for us in Genesis 5 as a careful record of the life span of those who trusted God. We stop to ponder just how our years would be recorded in light of our obedience and faith in the Lord Jesus Christ.*

"Without me ye can do nothing," Jesus said (John 15:5). If we have the Lord Jesus Christ, we know that our years will be called worthwhile rather than wasted. We are told in God's Word that we will have eternal recognition for the work which Jesus Christ has called each Christian to do.

Each builder's material will undergo a time of testing at Christ's Judgment Day. Everyone's work will be put through fire so that all can see whether or not it keeps its value. Then every workman who has built on the foundation, Jesus Christ, with the right materials, and whose work still stands, will get his pay. But if the house he has built burns up, he will have a great loss. He himself will be saved, but like a man escaping through a wall of flame.

We must ask ourselves if we have built on the foundation of the Lord Jesus Christ and used the materials which His Holy Spirit has given to us. "When the Holy Spirit controls our lives he will produce this kind of fruit in us: love, joy, peace, patience, kindness, goodness, faithfulness, gentleness, and self-control" (Galatians 5:22). Are these the materials that you have used in accomplishing the task which God has called you to through the Lord Jesus Christ? Will your work for Christ stand through eternity and be recognized by God with honor and reward because you have used the foundation of Jesus Christ and the materials which the Holy Spirit provided you with?

What is the work which God has called you to do?

As we look at the ages of Seth's descendants in Genesis 5, we realize that these early ancestors of ours were given many years by God. Seth lived 912 years (Genesis 5:8) and Methuselah lived 969 years (Genesis 5:27). Sydney Collett, in his book *All About the Bible*, shows that if only a portion of the race married, and if only a portion of those had children, the population of the earth was at least a million by the time Adam died, 930 years after his creation (Genesis 5:5). All of these men lived a long time, married, and had large families. In all probability, Adam saw five million of his own offspring on earth before he died.

Sin, disease, and a corrupt civilization had not yet had time to take its full toll upon the human mind and body, resulting in the deterioration of man and a shorter life span. It is also possible that the world

95

condition and the food was very different before the Flood. These conditions before the Flood could also account for the greater longevity of early man.

The Godly Line: Enoch to Lamech
Genesis 5:18-27

In Genesis 4 we met Enos who was the grandson of Adam through Cain. In Genesis 5:18 we meet Enoch who is one of the godliest men in the Bible. God does not want the two confused, so in the book of Jude he tells about Enoch the seventh from Adam, not the third from Adam (Jude 14).

In the whole line of Seth, Jared was the only one who outlived his son (Genesis 5:19). Yet, Jared must have had a happy heart when he saw how his son, Enoch, followed God. In Genesis 5:21 we read that Enoch was the father of Methuselah. We discover that this little baby grew to be the oldest man ever to live on earth.

God challenged Noah's faith by commanding him to build an ark which had three stories in it and the proportions of a large ship . . . . This challenge would be similar to God challenging us to build an eighteen thousand-ton ship!

When God commands the impossible, it is necessary that we have faith and the growth and maturity of faith to do this. God never asks us to do anything that He will not enable us to do. One of the greatest acts of faith in history was when Noah stretched out his hand and grasped the first tool to build the ark.

In Genesis 5:22,24 the phrase "Enoch walked with God" is repeated. Walking with God implies first, agreement. Enoch had faith and was reconciled to God through the sacrifice which was made in that day. He was one of the men of whom Hebrews 11:13 speaks of as those who "died in faith, not having received the promises, but having seen them afar off." They confessed their faith by their way of living and considered they were on their way to a "better country" with God.

Enoch's walk with God was not a casual stroll. His walking with God implies that he had surrendered his will to God. He wanted to walk according to God's plan for his life. To walk with God is not an honor peculiar to Enoch; it is open to any one of us who has received Christ. It means that we are conscious of God's presence at all times.

The walk of Genesis 5:22 was still going on in Genesis 5:24, three hundred years later. Jude tells us that Enoch preached (Jude 14,15). You can tell about his walk by the character of his preaching, for you discover that he used the word "ungodly" four times. The cousins (descendants of Cain) among whom he lived were ungodly, and he had no shyness in labeling them as such.

To walk with God is to learn to see things as He sees them. Enoch had a testimony of faith that pleased God (Hebrews 11:5). He may not have pleased his cousins, but he pleased God.

God tells us that Enoch did not see death (Hebrews 11:5). His family must have looked for him and they could not find him. That must have been the first great man hunt!

God took Enoch up to be with Him and he portrays a picture of how the Church (believers in Jesus Christ) will be called to God at the end of this age. Enoch was taken up alive, just as those believers will be who are living at the Lord's return. "[Those] who are alive and remain shall be caught up in the clouds to meet the Lord" (1 Thessalonians 4:1.

Enoch's family received no signal when he was called into the presence of God. But there will be a signal to Christians at that great day at the end of this age. First Thessalonians 4:16 tells us, "For the Lord Himself will descend from heaven with a shout, with the voice of the archangel, and with the trumpet of God." God planned for the Christian to know about this future thrilling event so that we could comfort each other with the promise of it (1 Thessalonians 4:18).

Today, God needs people who will walk with Him. He needs those who realize their weakness, and call upon God through the Lord Jesus Christ (Philippians 4:13; James 1:5). *We will receive strength from God if we choose to take time with Him and walk with Him in prayer and reading His Word.*

James 4:2 reminds you that you "have not, because ye ask not." How much time do you walk with God each day in prayer and reading His Word? Are you consciously practicing the presence of God as you go through your day? Do you recognize that God is with you as a Christian and He wants to help you with the smallest details of your life? Are you consciously sending up arrow prayers to Him during the day as you proceed about your business?

The Godly Line: Noah Genesis 5:28-32

In Genesis 5:28-29, we discover Lamech had a son, Noah, and gave him this name because it meant "comfort." Undoubtedly, Lamech had heard the preaching of his grandfather, Enoch, and the promise of judgment which Enoch had spoken of (Jude 15). Lamech still believed in God's promise that the seed of the woman would come to bruise the serpent's head (Genesis 3:15—the first promise of the Lord Jesus Christ in Scripture).

He called his son's name "comfort" because he was trusting in this promise. It is a comfort to us to know that God kept this promise in the giving of His Son, which He had planned before the foundation of the earth. These men looked forward to the promised Messiah, while we look back at the promised Messiah who came and who gave His life on the cross, who arose again from the dead to give us eternal life.

Just as Noah was a comfort to his family, so we have the Holy Spirit who is called the Comforter. The word "Comforter" means one who strengthens and helps. Noah was alone in an ungodly environment. Perhaps you, too, have special difficulties, sorrows or loneliness in your life today.

God gave us the Lord Jesus Christ who promised that the Holy Spirit would come to us when He ascended into heaven. "And I will pray the Father, and he shall give you another Comforter, that he may abide with you forever; even the Spirit of truth; whom the world cannot receive, because it seeth him not, neither knoweth him: but ye know him; for he dwelleth with you, and shall be in you. I will not leave you comfortless: I will come to you" (John 14:16-18).

Yes, God has given us Christ, who comes to us through the person of the Holy Spirit. Have you received the Comforter by receiving the Lord Jesus Christ in faith? God wants to strengthen and help you in your life by sending the Holy Spirit into your life as you come to His Son in faith. He will prove to you that He can completely satisfy any need in your life. Not only that, He will give you such an abundance of His strength, mercy, wisdom, and forgiveness that you will be able to pour out God's love to those who need it in your acquaintance. Are you willing to prove God by inviting Jesus Christ into your life and by making the choice to walk with Him daily this week?

The God of Judgment and the God of Love Genesis 6:1-14

We read in Genesis 6:2 that the sons of God saw the daughters of men and because they were fair, the sons of God took them for wives. No one fully understands the meaning of this mysterious passage. There are two explanations given by Bible scholars:

In one explanation of Genesis 6:1,2, Bible scholars believe the Hebrew text supports their view that the term "sons of God" in this passage refers to fallen angels (Jude 6) who assumed human form in order to marry mortal women. For their abnormal crime, God is said to have imprisoned them forever (2 Peter 2:4,5). "God angels" do assume human form at the bidding of God in several places in the Bible (Genesis 19:1). Thus, theologians who hold this viewpoint believe that the fallen angels likewise assumed human form in order to marry the daughters of men.

A second explanation is that the "sons of God" represents the godly line of Seth (Genesis 4:25—5:32) and the "daughters of men" represents the sinful line of Cain (Genesis 4:16-24). They believe that godly men who married wicked women caused Seth's descendants to become equally as wicked as those of Cain. Scholars holding to this belief point out that Jesus said in Matthew 22:30 that angels "neither marry, nor are given in marriage." As we consider this explanation we can certainly see that it affirms a great principle of the Bible that corruption of the family leads to corruption of the nation. Also 2 Corinthians 6:14 teaches us that a Christian should not marry a non-Christian.

In Genesis 6:3 we might find mention of the Holy Spirit as the Lord says, "My spirit shall not always strive with man." Sin had been increasing on the earth. We read "the wickedness of man was great in the earth" (Genesis 6:5), "the earth . . . was corrupt before God" (Genesis 6:11,12), and "the earth was filled with violence" (Genesis 6:11).

God would judge the earth with a flood and completely annihilate the corrupt race, but would preserve the seed of the "righteous" Noah, who was saved from destruction through his faith in God's warning and promise of salvation. We see God's tender love and compassion for man in Genesis 6:3 as He waits 120 years before bringing judgment. First Peter 3:20 says, "the longsuffering of God waited in the days of Noah, while the ark was preparing." This leads us to believe that it must have taken approximately 120 years for Noah to build the ark and to preach repentance to his generation before the flood of God's judgment fell.

In 2 Peter 3:9 we read, "The Lord is not slow about his promise, as some count slowness, but is patient toward you, not wishing for any to perish but for all to come to repentance." God is the same yesterday, today, and forever. He is still waiting for people to come in faith to Him today through His Son, the Lord Jesus Christ.

The Bible does warn us against hardening our hearts as those in the time of Noah did. In Romans 2:4, "Don't you realize how patient he is being with you? Or don't you care? Can't you see that he has been waiting all this time without punishing you, to give you time to turn from your sin? His kindness is meant to lead you to repentance." How is it with your heart? Have you hardened your heart?

99

In Genesis 6:6 it looked as if God were changing His mind. He was really teaching that sin brought the display of His wrath through these events. We see the result of sin in Genesis 6:7 by the words, "I will destroy man."Yet as we see judgment in verse 7, we see God's grace in verse 8. *Grace is the unearned love from God which Noah received. Noah was "a just man" (Genesis 6:9) and though in this same verse he is called "perfect," it does not mean that he was sinless. God was looking at him through Christ. It was by faith in God (Hebrews 11:7) and trust in God's Word that Noah could be called righteous.*

Noah had personal sins, but God forgave him because of his faith. Noah walked with God just as his ancestor, Enoch, had. God revealed His future plans to him in Genesis 6:14 by saying, "Make thee an ark." He told Noah that He would bring judgment upon the earth in Genesis 6:13 and 17. He promised Noah safety in the ark. Noah gave evidence of his faith as he was obedient in his daily life for 120 years. He patiently built the ark in the midst of scoffing men around him. How they must have laughed as he proclaimed God's Word of the coming judgment! He was building an ark and speaking of a flood that would destroy life!

God Tells Noah How to Make the Ark
Genesis 6:14-22

God challenged Noah's faith by commanding him to build an ark which had three stories in it and the proportions of a large ship. The length was to be six times the width and ten times the height. One cubit equals eighteen inches, if you wish to figure the measurement of the ark. This challenge would be similar to God challenging us to build an eighteen thousand-ton ship!

When God commands the impossible, it is necessary that we have faith and the growth and maturity of faith to do this. God never asks us to do anything that He will not enable us to do. One of the greatest acts of faith in history was when Noah stretched out his hand and grasped the first tool to build the ark. Noah followed God's direction which provided for plenty of room for various species of animals and their food plus living space for Noah and his family. God provided the right plan for building the ark, and He provided Noah with the material and the strength to build it with. *"God is our refuge and strength, a.very present help in trouble" (Psalm 46:1). "He giveth power to the faint; and to them that have no might he increaseth strength" (Isaiah 40:29).*

Surely we do not live in a world more evil than Noah did! Surely our problems can be no greater than Noah's! Surely our fears concerning our children can be no greater than Noah's fears for his own children! God preserved Noah and his family because Noah trusted in Him and obeyed His Word.

We can trust God today and obey His Word as Noah did. "In him we live, and move, and have our being" (Acts 17:28). *Will you trust God this week, and be conscious of His help moment by moment?* Will you seek to obey Him as you read His Word and listen to Him in prayer this week?

The ark that saved Noah from perishing by God's judgment and preserved him as he lived upon this earth is a picture of the Lord Jesus Christ who has come to save us from judgment. In the ark of salvation (the Lord Jesus Christ) we are kept safely by God. Those who are outside of Christ will suffer inevitable destruction (John 3:36). Have you chosen forgiveness and safety by inviting the Lord Jesus Christ into your life?

Noah was obedient to God. In Genesis 6:14 he is told to put pitch upon the ark. *The Hebrew word for pitch is the same word for "atonement." There would be no leak in the ark, for the pitch kept the water from entering in. Similarly, the judgment of God does not touch the believer because the death of the Lord Jesus Christ stands between the believer and the wrath of God forever.* A great beauty of God's love is expressed in this verse.

God gives Noah the exact proportions for the ark in Genesis 6:15. A Christian engineer, lecturing before a war college meeting at Annapolis, told the admiral that for centuries men had built ships in various proportions. He went on to say that British naval architects had found the formula for the battleship, *Dreadnought,* and since that time all naval construction had followed the proportions of this ship because it was scientifically perfect. This Christian engineer then said that the proportions of the *Dreadnought* were exactly those of the ark!

The ark is often pictured as a huge ship with one window. Probably this verse (Genesis 6:16) means there was an open "gallery" all the way around the ark. There was to be only one door in the ark, symbolizing that there is only one way to God. "I am the way, the truth, and the life: no man cometh unto the Father, but by me" (John 14:6).

Inside the ark, Noah and his family were safe from all the floods of judgment. When we are "in Christ" we are safe also. The three decks, which provided space for everyone who needed to be in the ark, point to the fact that there is room enough for all to come to God through the Lord Jesus Christ. These three decks provided ample room for all of the animals, Noah, and his family.

We see God's promise in Genesis 6:18. God never acts by whim,

101

for He has an eternal plan. God always keeps His covenant and promises to us.

God planned for two of every living thing to be taken to the ark, including fowl, cattle, and creeping thing (Genesis 6:19,20). This verse specifically mentions "male and female" to emphasize God's intent to preserve His creation of animal life. Noah also was to take food for all the animals as well as for his family.

In Genesis 6:22 we read, "Thus did Noah; according to all that God commanded, so did he." True obedience consists not only of doing what one is told, but doing *all* that you are told to do. Disobedience could have been as dangerous as building the ark without a floor or without putting pitch on it. The water would have come through and the rest of the work would have been spoiled.

As the Holy Spirit reveals God's plan for our lives as Christians, we need to be obedient to God. *If God speaks to you in some special way this week through His Word and prayer, will you find joy in obeying Him as Noah did?*

Study Questions

Before you begin your study this week:
1. Pray and ask God to speak to you through His Holy Spirit each day.
2. Use only your Bible for your answers.
3. Write your answers and the verses you have used.
4. Challenge questions are for those who have the time and wish to do them.
5. Personal questions are to be shared with your study group only if you wish to share.
6. As you study look for a verse to memorize this week. Write it down, carry it with you, tack it to your bulletin board, tape it to the dashboard of your car. Make a real effort to learn the verse and its reference.

FIRST DAY: Read all of the notes and look up all of the Scriptures.

1. What was a helpful or new thought from the overview of Genesis 5 and 6?

2. What personal application did you select to apply to your own life this week?

SECOND DAY: Read all of Genesis 7, concentrating on verses 1-16.

1. What new fact do you learn about the number of animals to be brought into the ark in Genesis 7:2,3?

2 a. How long were Noah and his family to be inside the ark before it started to rain?

b. (Personal) God kept His promise to send rain, but Noah had to wait seven days inside the ark first. Are you praying about something and claiming God's promise, yet still waiting for His answer? If possible, share an experience of waiting and praying and tell how God answered.

3 a. **Challenge:** Read the following verses which speak of trusting God and put them in your own words.

Proverbs 16:20

Jeremiah 17:5,7

Psalm 3:3,5

Psalm 16:1,11

b. Do you think these verses describe Noah's attitude while he waited in the ark for the rain to come?

c. (Personal) What about you? Do they describe your attitude as you wait on God in prayer in some problem?

d. Which verse would you like to incorporate into your life attitude this week?

4. What was Noah's attitude toward God, which should be the Christian's constant desire? See Genesis 7:5.

5 a. How long did it rain and from what two sources did the flood waters come?

b. Who shut the door of the ark when all had gone into it? Give verse.

6. If you are surrounded by difficulties and overwhelming circumstances right now, are you letting God "shut you" into His care so that these things cannot harm you? Are you allowing God to give you His peace in your circumstances? See Psalm 31:19 and John 14:27 if you need help from the Lord Jesus in your circumstances. Claim these promises for yourself today!

THIRD DAY: Read Genesis 7:17 through Genesis 8:1-19.

1. Name the things that were destroyed by the flood because of God's judgment on man's sin. Give verses.

2 a. What does the New Testament say about the penalty for sin in Romans 6:23?

b. What wonderful gift is also mentioned in Romans 6:23? Who makes it possible for you to receive this gift by faith?

3. **Challenge:** Think of Noah safe in the ark. Because he trusted God he was not punished for sin as were the rest of the human race at this time. The ark is a symbol of the safety that Jeşus Christ offers us as we invite Him into our lives to be our Savior and Lord. Put into your own words how you would explain this great truth to someone else, using any Scripture you know. Suggestions for Scripture—John 3:16,17; Matthew 1:21; Romans 3:23; Romans 5:8.

105

4 a. How did God remember Noah's faith and deliver him safely? Summarize Genesis 8:1-3.

b. Assuming that a month has approximately 30 days, about how many months did the flood last? See Genesis 7:24; 8:3.

5 a. What two birds did Noah send out from the ark? Which one returned with something, and what did God show Noah by this? Give verses.

b. What did God tell Noah to do after Noah had seen that the earth was dry? Give verses.

6 a. Did Noah obey God's words to him?

b. (Personal) Noah believed God's Word and obeyed. What are you doing to hear God's Word and then obey it?

c. Challenge: The following verses will help you to know the importance of hearing God's Word and being obedient as Noah was. Check your favorite verse. Put the verses into your own words if possible.

Psalm 119:11

John 8:47

John 5:24

2 Timothy 3:16,17

FOURTH DAY: Read Genesis 8:20-22.

1. What was the first thing Noah did when he and his family left the ark?

2. Do you think that all of Noah's family participated in this "thank you service" to God? Give reasons why.

3. **Challenge:** Genesis 8:21 says that God "smelled a sweet savour" of the sacrifice. This means that He was pleased with the worship which took place at this altar which Noah built. Read 2 Corinthians 2:14,15 (in a modern English translation, if possible). According to these verses:

   a. Who is it that causes a Christian to triumph in any difficult situation?

   b. What "sweet perfume" is the Christian to share or reflect wherever he goes?

   c. What is the only sweet, wholesome fragrance in our lives that makes us acceptable to God?

   d. If we depended on our own goodness and kindness, this

107

would not be a sweet fragrance to God. What would our own goodness and kindness "smell like" and "look like," if they were as described in Isaiah 64:6?

4. (Personal) God was pleased that Noah when he got off the ark built an altar to worship Him. Before you start your day, do you take time in the morning to praise and worship the Lord—even if it is just to thank the Lord for the new day and the rest He provided for you during the night?

5. (Personal) Have you set aside a certain time during each day (preferably early before the hurry of the day begins) to meet God at an "altar" (a place set apart) for prayer and study of His Word? Please record when and how you do this and the joy that it brings you. Share with your discussion group if possible.

6. Noah led his family in a worship experience. Are you helping anyone to worship God—at your place of business, in your home, or in your community? If possible, explain how Christ by the Holy Spirit has led you and what methods you have used successfully.

FIFTH DAY: Read Genesis 9:1-19.

1. What did God promise never to do again in Genesis 8:21?

2. As a promise of this covenant in Genesis 8:21, what did God say He would put in the sky to remind man down through the ages of His covenant promise to Noah? Read Genesis 9:11-17. Pick out key phrases and give verses.

3. Not only would man look at the rainbow as God's promise never to send a flood again, but who else would be looking at it? Give verse.

108

4 a. Who were the three sons of Noah?

b. How was the earth populated after the Flood? See Genesis 9:1,7,19.

5. What new thing did God allow man to eat after the Flood, according to Genesis 9:2,3? How did this strain man's relationship with these creatures?

6. Why did God say a man or an animal must die for the crime of killing a man? See Genesis 9:5,6.

SIXTH DAY: Read Genesis 9:20-29.

1. What did Noah do in Genesis 9:20,21 which emphasized what God taught in Romans 3:23?

2. Even Noah was not perfect, though he walked with God (Genesis 6:8,9). Who was the only perfect One who walked this earth? See 1 Peter 2:21,22; 1 John 3:5; and Hebrews 4:14,15.

3. What kindness did Shem and Japheth show their father in his humiliation?

4. Ham had discovered the nakedness of his father, but what did he do instead of covering him up in his humiliation?

5. What was the result of Ham's lack of love and consideration for his father?

6 a. (Personal) How do you react when you discover that a person has done something which is displeasing to God? Do you try and help that person through prayer and loving deeds, or do you tell everyone about his problems and gloat over him?

   b. What do the following verses from God's Word advise you to do in such situations?

   Proverbs 21:23

   Proverbs 17:9

   Proverbs 10:12

   1 John 4:10,11

   c. Which Scripture did you choose to commit to memory this week?

GOD REMEMBERS AND BLESSES THOSE WHO OBEY HIM

GENESIS 7-9

Study Notes

Adam and Eve were put out of the Garden of Eden, and were told what would happen because each had sinned. Now as we study Genesis 7—9 we see that God would have to do something to show the people of Noah's generation how much He hated sin. "The Lord said, I will destroy man whom I have created from the face of the earth; both man, and beast, and the creeping thing, and the fowls of the air; for it repenteth me that I have made them" (Genesis 6:7).

Noah: A Man Who Pleased God

Out of all of the thousands of people in the world at this time only one man and his family pleased God. The man's name was Noah. *The Bible says, "all have sinned" (Romans 3:23), so we know that Noah was not sinless. But he trusted and loved God, and so we read, "But Noah found grace [divine favor] in the eyes of the Lord" (Genesis 6:8). God planned to save Noah and his family and to make a new beginning if Noah would obey Him.*

Before God judged the wickedness of the world, He spoke to Noah and warned him of the judgment to come. God asked Noah to

111

do some strange work. He told Noah there would be a flood, and that he was to make an ark to save himself, his family and two of every kind of animal from death by the flood waters. Noah must have had difficulty understanding what a flood was, but he trusted God and was willing to obey, although he didn't understand all that God said.

Are you in difficult circumstances today? Are there things in your circumstances that you do not understand? Are you willing to trust God and obey Him as He leads you in these circumstances through His Word and prayer? This is what Noah did.

Noah: A Man Who Obeyed God

God told Noah exactly how to build this great ark; what kind of material to use, how long and how wide to make it, and where to put the ventilators and the door. The ark, calculated according to figures today, was 450 feet long, 75 feet wide, and 45 feet high. This size has been calculated by determining that one cubit equals approximately 18 inches. It took Noah about 120 years to build this large ship (Genesis 6:3).

God designed and planned the ark, and Noah was secure in it. Yet, there was plenty for Noah to do. His work was cut out for him. To care for and feed all the animals and to keep things in order would have been quite a task. So, too, the believer in Christ, safe in the "ark of salvation" by his faith in the Lord Jesus Christ, has a responsibility and duty to care for those who have been entrusted to his care.

Many people wonder how the ark could have held all the animals that God told Noah to take aboard, but this great ark built more than 5,000 years ago, was as big as a modern destroyer today. It was more than a block and a half long and could carry as much freight as a freight train thirteen and a half miles long! Imagine how the people must have laughed at Noah and his sons as they were building this strange boat.

Yet, what an honor it was to be chosen from a crowd and given a task to do for God. Noah had great courage. He kept on building while the people laughed at him

Has anyone ever laughed at you for being obedient to God? If so, follow Noah's example and be sure to obey God in such cases.

112

The Lord tells Noah: "Come" Genesis 7

God could never have told Noah to "come into the ark" (Genesis 7:1) if Noah had not been obedient to God. He listened to God and then he obeyed. "Thus did Noah; according to all that God commanded him" (Genesis 6:22). This is such an important verse that God repeats it in Genesis 7:5, "And Noah did according unto all that the Lord commanded him."

Wouldn't it be wonderful if this could be said about you? *You must not only listen and learn what God wants you to do, but also do it. As you listen and learn, and as the Holy Spirit speaks to you, are you putting into practice what you hear and learn?*

There was only one place of safety for Noah, and that was in the ark. Those outside the ark disobeyed God and perished in the flood. The ark is a picture of what Christ is to us today. It points us to the Lord Jesus Christ and our need to invite Him into our lives (Revelation 3:20).

The ark was a safe vessel. There could be no storm violent enough to cause it to sink. *The designer and architect Himself was present in the ark with its occupants.* The record speaks for itself as we read in Genesis 7:1, "And the Lord said unto Noah, Come thou and all thy house into the ark."

Notice the word, COME. This is the very first time the word "come" occurs in the Bible. God did not say to Noah, "Now the ark is ready and it is safe, so don't hesitate to GO in, for I will be outside watching over you to prevent any harm." This would have been enough for Noah, but this was not what God did. He went into the ark first, and then invited Noah and his family to come and join Him. With God in the ark, Noah was safe. God's own presence was a guarantee of the great safety that Noah and his family would know.

A chief pilot of an international airliner who flew over the sea and mountains on his route was asked one day, "Don't you find the responsibility of carrying over a hundred passengers in your great plane a strain on you? How does it feel to realize that you are responsible for all those lives behind you?"

This pilot just completed 25 years of flying millions of miles with all these people. His answer to the question was, "I never think of the safety of those passengers; I only think of my own safety." He was not indifferent to the safety of his passengers, but he knew their safety depended on his own safety. The best protection he could give his passengers was to be alert every minute to his job as pilot of the plane.

This example can never fully illustrate how God protected the ark through the flood waters, but it carries the lesson that with God in the

113

ark, Noah was safe. *This lesson was also that the disciples of Jesus had not yet learned in the great storm in Matthew, chapter 8. They came to the sleeping Jesus, and cried: "Lord, save us: we perish" (Matthew 8:25). When Jesus Christ is in the ship, it cannot sink!*

The occupants of the ark had nothing to do with operating the ark. Evidently the ark had no sails, no motor or engine, no oars, no rudder, and no pilot house. God Himself directed the course of that great ship. The common idea that the ark just drifted aimlessly upon the roaring waters is far from the truth. It was carefully piloted and steered by the hand of Him who said, "Come in." The ark was piloted to a safe place, Mt. Ararat (Genesis 8:4), where God safely landed it.

So, too, when we trust Christ and come into the ark of safety by our faith in Him we are not left to drift aimlessly upon the tide of life. Every moment we have the Lord Jesus Christ with us, guiding us. Our job is to listen to the Holy Spirit and be willing to follow obediently. Jesus

When we come to the Lord Jesus Christ, when we hear Him say, "Come," we need to spend time with Him. We can get to know Him through prayer and study of His Word. After we have been Christians for a time, the Lord will say, "Go forth," and send us to someone in need.

Christ said, "I will not leave you comfortless: I will come to you" (John 14:18). "And I will pray the Father, and he shall give you another Comforter, that he may abide with you forever" (John 14:16).

God designed and planned the ark, and Noah was secure in it. Yet, there was plenty for Noah to do. His work was cut out for him. To care for and feed all the animals and to keep things in order would have been quite a task. So, too, the believer in Christ, safe in the "ark of salvation" by his faith in the Lord Jesus Christ, has a responsibility and duty to care for those who have been entrusted to his care.

Paul says, "Work out your own salvation with fear and trembling. For it is *God which worketh in you* both to will and to do of his good pleasure" (Philippians 2:12,13). *God has a work for you to do in this world. He wants to accomplish this work through you as He empowers you by the Holy Spirit.*

Are you willing to be open to hear God speak to you? And then are you willing to obey and do the work He has planned for you to do? Noah was obedient. Will you be obedient?

While the door of the ark was open, those who believed God's Word could come in. But once the door was shut, no one could come into the ark. However, there is one little phrase in the account which

114

is too often overlooked. "And they that went in, went in male and female of all flesh, as God commanded him; *AND THE LORD SHUT HIM IN*" (Genesis 7:16). God did not say, "Now Noah, shut the door and slide the bar." No, the Lord does not place the safety of His own in the hands of men. He Himself snaps the lock.

There was only one ark. God did not provide a fleet of arks and say, "You may have your choice." There are religions without number, but there is only one way of salvation. Jesus said, "I am the door: by me if any man enter in, he shall be saved" (John 10:9). Have you entered into God's family by the one door, the Lord Jesus Christ? How are you helping others to find this door?

Noah did not have to chase after the animals to catch them and bring them into the ark. God in His goodness sent them to him as we read in Genesis 6:20, "Two of every sort shall come unto thee, to keep them alive."

In Genesis 7:2 we read that God further instructed Noah to take seven pairs of every clean beast into the ark and only one pair of the unclean beasts into the ark. By clean, God meant animals that were acceptable for sacrifice. He could not have accepted "unclean" animals for a sacrifice. Leviticus 11 describes the unclean animals.

Only ten kinds of animals were clean. God wanted more of them brought on the ark for they needed to multiply more rapidly since they would be sacrificed upon the altar for the sins of Noah and his family when the ark landed. If they had only one male and one female of the clean beasts these animals would have been extinct at that point.

In Genesis 7:4 God told Noah that for seven days it would not rain, and then He would send rain for forty days and forty nights which would destroy every living substance upon the face of the earth and everything that had breath of life. Noah was 600 years old when the waters of the Flood were upon the earth. And in Genesis 7:7 we find that Noah went into the ark with his wife, and his sons' wives, and his sons. For Noah to go into the ark before the rains had started and to wait inside the ark for God to act was a tremendous act of faith. The people around must have thought that Noah's folly had reached its climax!

When we pray about a problem, we can trust God in the same way that Noah did. We may not see our answer immediately. But we know that God is faithful and has promised to answer the prayers of the Christian who asks according to His will. Have you taken the step of faith to pray about your problems? Why not come to God in the name of Jesus Christ today and trust Him as Noah did?

In Genesis 7:11 we find the two ways God sent the flood waters upon the earth. "The same day were all the fountains of the great deep broken up, and the windows of heaven were opened." God

115

allowed rain from the heavens, and water rose up from the earth itself. This deluge continued for forty days and forty nights until in Genesis 7:19 we read that all of the high hills were under water and, in Genesis 7:20, "Fifteen cubits upward did the waters prevail; and the mountains were covered."

Many people have wondered if the fish died in the Flood. Genesis 7:22 says that all in whose nostrils was the breath of life, all that was on dry land died. Since fish have gills—not nostrils—and can live in the water, we assume from this statement that the fish lived during the flood. To our knowledge, Noah was given no instructions to build water tanks and carry fish on the ark. In Genesis 7:24 we read that the flood waters were upon the earth 150 days. Assuming that a month is approximately 30 days, we presume the flood lasted about five months.

God Remembers Noah Genesis 8

"And God remembered Noah," (Genesis 8:1). If God had not remembered Noah, God would not have been God. "The Lord knows those who are his" (2 Timothy 2:19). "If we are faithless, He remains faithful; for He cannot deny Himself" (2 Timothy 2:13). God always remembers His own. You are never forgotten by God.

God remembered Noah by causing a wind to pass over the earth, and the waters began to dry up. The fountains of the deep and the windows of heaven were stopped (Genesis 8:2). God guided the ark to Mt. Ararat where it rested in the seventh month on the seventeenth day (Genesis 8:4).

First Noah sent out a raven which never returned, and then the dove, which returned to him when it found no rest for the sole of its foot (Genesis 8:9). He waited seven days and then sent the dove out again. This time the dove returned with an olive leaf, which indicated that things were beginning to grow on the earth again.

Noah waited seven days and then sent forth the dove once again. This time the dove did not return, so in Genesis 8:13 we find that Noah removed the covering of the ark and when he looked out he saw dry ground. Again God spoke to Noah and told him this time to "go forth" or leave the ark (Genesis 8:16).

When we come to the Lord Jesus Christ, when we hear Him say, "Come," we need to spend time with Him. We can get to know Him through prayer and study of His Word. After we have been Christians for a time, the Lord will say, "Go forth," and send us to someone in need.

Are you listening? Have you heard God's Word to you, Christian?

116

Has He said, "Go forth"? Are you being obedient as Noah was?

The first thing Noah did after leaving the ark was to build an altar unto the Lord (Genesis 8:20). He then took of every clean beast and of every clean fowl and offered a burnt offering on the altar. Blood had to be shed for the forgiveness of sin.

The world had been judged, but the evil nature of Adam had gone into the ark, and the evil nature of Adam had come out of the ark. "Wherefore, as by one man [Adam] sin entered into the world, and death by sin; and so death passed upon all men, for that all have sinned" (Romans 5:12). Noah knew that an animal had to be killed as a substitute for his own self because of his sin. Noah wanted to establish fellowship with God and this is why he built an altar immediately, and sacrificed these animals for the forgiveness of his sin.

These animal sacrifices pointed to the final sacrifice of Jesus Christ upon the cross for our sins. Now we see why seven of the clean beasts were taken into the ark. Life in the new world after the Flood was to be based on faith in the substitute atonement—blood had to be shed for the forgiveness of sins.

There was but one way to God as there always will be but one way. Today the only way is the blood of Christ which brings us into fellowship with God. "But now in Christ Jesus ye who sometimes were far off are made nigh by the blood of Christ" (Ephesians 2:13).

In simple fashion Noah was showing the Lord's death in this pageant. In Genesis 8:21, "The Lord smelled a sweet savour." God was not looking upon the actual altar and sacrifice, but upon Calvary and the Lord Jesus Christ dying there for sinners.

At this point God promised that He would never again curse the earth with a flood. *The Flood was a strong object lesson, and there was no need to repeat it.* As long as the earth shall remain, there will be "seedtime and harvest, and cold and heat, and summer and winter, and day and night." God promised this in Genesis 8:22.

God Blesses Noah and His Sons Genesis 9

In Genesis 9:1 God blessed Noah and his sons. Adam was the head of the race, but Noah had a new beginning. This new start is marked by a blessing. God instructed Noah and his sons to be fruitful, and multiply, and replenish the earth. This instruction does not merely refer to the reproduction of the species, but to fruitfulness in every good work before God.

"That the way you live will always please the Lord and honor him, so that you will always be doing good, kind things for others, while all the time you are learning to know God better and better . . . that you will be filled with his mighty, glorious strength so that you can keep

117

going no matter what happens—always full of the joy of the Lord" (Colossians 1:10,11).

We are not put here on earth to live according to our own whim, but to live in accordance with God's plan for our lives. He has provided His mighty glorious strength in the Christian by the power of the Holy Spirit to accomplish all that He wants us to do. Are you allowing God to have His way in your life? Are you fruitful in every good work before God?

Secondly, God assured Noah of his safety and his power by putting a fear and a dread of man into the heart of all the animals (Genesis 9:2). This would be a natural fear, as God moved on to say that He was giving man meat for his food from now on, as well as the green herb that was supplied as food before the Flood (Genesis 9:3).

We find a reference to capital punishment in Genesis 9:5,6. God required that a beast or a man who destroyed another human life must be killed. To God, the human being is sacred. "For in the image of God made he man" (Genesis 9:6). *As we look at our fellow human beings, we need to remember that we are looking at persons who are created after the image of God. We need to respect people of every race and color.*

God made a covenant with Noah and his descendants. He promised that never again would there be a universal flood upon the earth (Genesis 9:9-12). As a reminder, He said He would set a rainbow in the clouds. When the storm beats fiercely upon the earth, a beautiful rainbow reminds us that God promised never again to destroy the earth by a flood.

It was out of the clouds that the rain came, yet it was on their retreating shadows that God placed the beautiful rainbow of promise. *So in our lives, as we are deluged with billows of affliction, God wisely designs to braid into our troubles a rainbow of some kind to remind us of His love.* Are you trusting His promises to triumph over your circumstances?

"But now the Lord who created you, Oh Israel, says, Don't be afraid, for I have ransomed you; I have called you by name; you are mine. When you go through deep waters and great trouble, I will be with you. When you go through rivers of difficulty, you will not drown! When you walk through the fire of oppression, you will not be burned up—the flames will not consume you" (Isaiah 43:1,2). Are you looking for God's rainbow today?

In Genesis 9:20 we discover that Noah became a "husbandman" and planted a vineyard. In the next verse we find that he drank of the wine of his vineyard and became drunk. He was uncovered inside his tent. Yet Noah is recorded as a "preacher of righteousness" in 2 Peter 2:5. Noah is a great illustration of the fact that many men in the Bible who were strong for God when they were young departed far from

118

the will of God when they were older. It is a warning that past work does not furnish power for future victory.

The Bible is honest concerning Noah. Through his story, we become increasingly aware that the godliest of men are not immune from the temptations of sin. Many times after a particular spiritual victory, when one is apt to let down, Satan takes advantage and tempts us. This truth can be a warning to Christians today to keep close to the Lord Jesus Christ and to keep short accounts with God (1 John 1:9).

Alcohol is a large influence on our society today and social drinking is one of the main problems. Alcohol causes much suffering, crime, and juvenile delinquency. *Alcoholism is ranked third (behind heart disease and cancer) as North America's most serious and costly public health problem.*

If people learn the habit of drinking in our home and then go on to become alcoholics, it would be our encouragement which stumbled them. We would be held guilty before God for setting the wrong example. Each Christian needs to pray carefully concerning social drinking in our day and ask the Holy Spirit what is pleasing to God in this matter.

In Genesis 9:22, Ham saw his father's nakedness and, instead of trying to help him, told his brothers about it. Shem and Japheth did what every Christian should do when he sees someone in trouble. They quietly covered their father without even looking at him.

Because Ham told of his father's weakness as if it were news, rather than respecting him as a father in his weakness, he was cursed (Genesis 9:25). Some people believe that all of the black races are under a curse, simply because they are descended from Ham, whose name means "black." This notion is not true. Only Canaan and his descendants were cursed. Any attempt to make black skin the fulfillment of Ham's curse is prejudice in the extreme and certainly without basis in the Bible.

The Flood: Local or Universal?

Two main viewpoints concerning the Flood exist among Christians. One group believes that the Flood was a localized flood in the area where Adam and Eve lived. They believe that the Bible described the area that was inhabited by the early civilization of Noah's day. They feel that there was no need for a worldwide deluge, since the Flood over the inhabited part of the earth would have been sufficient to bring judgment and an end to life.

The second viewpoint is of a universal flood which covered the whole earth. The fact that God commanded Noah to take in representatives of all the land animals suggests the idea that the Flood was

119

universal. A local flood would not have involved all the land animals. Another reason that would lead one to believe that it was a universal flood is the use of the word "every" in describing the destruction of the Flood. For instance, Genesis 7:4, "every living substance," Genesis 8:1, "every living thing," Genesis 7:21, "all flesh died that moved upon the earth," and again in Genesis 7:19, "all the high hills" were covered. This last reference does not necessarily mean that all our high mountains today were covered by the Flood.

Also, because water seeks its own level, it is difficult to imagine water being at a greater height in Asia Minor than anywhere else on the earth. Great theologians differ in their view of whether it was a local or universal flood. *One day in heaven God will reveal this to us. In the meantime let us not quarrel over the subject, but let us be busy seeking to glorify the Lord and to know His will for our lives.*

Noah: An example for Us All

Let us again look for a moment at Genesis 8:20-22, and note that the first thing which Noah did was "build an altar to the Lord" after he had shepherded all the animals and all his family onto the dry ground. *Noah set an example for his family in leading them in worship and being thankful to God.*

What is the first thing you do in the morning when you open your eyes? A wise habit is to start your day with reading God's Word and Bible study. This course provides a ready plan for you to do this.

Noah also set an example for his family by saying "thank you" to God, and offering sacrifices upon the altar for his sins. *We need to be an example to our family and to our friends, and to encourage them to worship God in this same way.* God will be pleased with our worship and with the sweet perfume of Christ's love which we reflect to others.

Study Questions

Before you begin your study this week:
1. Pray and ask God to speak to you through His Holy Spirit each day.
2. Use only your Bible for answers.
3. Write your answers and the verses you have used.
4. Challenge questions are for those who have the time and wish to do them.
5. Personal questions are to be shared with your study group only if you wish to share.
6. As you study look for a verse to memorize this week. Write it down, carry it with you, tack it to your bulletin board, tape it to the dashboard of your car. Make a real effort to learn the verse and its reference.

FIRST DAY: Read all of the notes and look up all the Scriptures.

1. What was a helpful or new thought from the overview of Genesis 7-9?

2. What personal application did you select to apply to your own life this week?

SECOND DAY: Read all of Genesis 10.

1. Whose family tree does this record?

2. **Challenge:** Since this was after the Flood (Genesis 10:1), do you believe that these were the ancestors of the whole human race? Give scriptural reasons for your answer.

3. Who was the mighty hunter mentioned in this chapter? Where was the beginning of his kingdom? Give verses.

4. What interesting thing happened during the lifetime of Peleg? Give verse.

5 a. What interesting parallel developments do you find among the sons of Japheth, Ham and Shem in verses 5, 20 and 31?

b. According to Genesis 10:2-5, what was the general name given to all of Japheth's descendants?

6 a. Challenge: Genesis 10 gives us the historical flow of Noah's family from generation to generation after they left the ark. If you belong to Jesus Christ you are in God's family (John 14:6). A family has certain responsibilities. What do the following Scriptures tell you about this? Try to put them into your own words and apply them to your life.

Deuteronomy 4:9,10

1 Timothy 3:4,5

Proverbs 22:6

b. (Personal) Which of these verses meant the most to you? Give the reason for this. Share with your group, if possible.

THIRD DAY: Read all of Genesis 11.

1 a. What did all of Noah's descendants have in common at this time?

b. When Noah and his family left the ark after the Flood, which direction did they travel and where did they first settle?

c. What natural resources in the land provided building materials for their homes?

2 a. What were the reasons why the people decided to build the Tower of Babel? Give verse.

b. Read Genesis 9:1 and 9:7 to determine if these people were following God's plan for their lives or their own human desires.

c. (Personal) Will you ask the Lord Jesus Christ to give you His attitudes so that you, too, will want God's plan for your life this week?

3 a. How did God stop these people from carrying out their plans? Give verses.

b. **Challenge:** Are you worried about the evil that seems to be flourishing on our earth today? Do men seem to be making plans opposite of what God would desire for the world? What encouragement do you find in Genesis 11:1-9 for our world today?

4 a. **Challenge:** What word in Genesis 11:7 points out that God is a Trinity?

b. **Challenge:** The following verses also reveal God as a Trinity (three persons in one). Look up each one and write it down.

Matthew 28:19

Luke 3:22

Titus 3:4-6

5. The scattering of the people which occurs in Genesis 11:7-9 probably happened during the time that Peleg (Shem's descendant) lived. What phrase in Genesis 10:25 would suggest a scattering of people?

6. Who were two descendants of Shem whose names started with the letter A? See Genesis 11:10-32. Give verses.

FOURTH and FIFTH DAYS: Read all of Genesis 12:1-9.
(Note Abram and Abraham are the same person.)

1 a. According to Acts 7:4, what area did Abram live in before God asked him to move? What is this land called in Genesis 11:31?

b. According to Genesis 12:1, what was Abram to leave beside his homeland?

c. What did God promise Abram if he would obey Him? Give verse.

d. (Personal) In Genesis 12:2 God told Abram that he would be a blessing to others if he obeyed Him. Have you ever experienced obeying God and by your obedience found that He has blessed others with your life? Write down any such experience and share with your discussion group, if possible.

2 a. What was the name of the land that God promised to Abram? Give verse.

   b. Who did Abram take with him? Read Genesis 11:31 and Genesis 12:5.

3 a. When Abram arrived in Canaan, to whom did God promise this land? Give verse.

   b. How did Abram express his complete faith in God's promise to him even though he had no children?

   c. (Personal) God wants people who are willing to obey Him. He will provide all that you need for what He asks you to do. Are you willing to "listen" to God this week in your prayer time and as you read His Word, and then are you willing to step out by faith as Abram did in obedience?

4. **Challenge:** Think of how hard it must have been for Abram to leave his home for a strange new land. Read Mark 8:34-36 and use these verses to help you describe how a Christian today should be just as willing to follow what Jesus Christ asks of him.

5. Write down all you can learn about faith and about Abram and Sarah's (Sarai's) faith in Hebrews 11:6,8-12.

6 a. Christ also promises many wonderful things to those who will receive Him in faith. Read the following verses to discover some of these promises and check your favorites.

John 14:27

Romans 8:35,37-39

Matthew 4:18,19

b. (Personal) Which of these verses would you like to claim for your life this week?

SIXTH DAY: Read Genesis 12:10-20 and Genesis 13.

1 a. Why did Abram have to leave Canaan and where did he go? Give verses.

b. **Challenge:** Relate the sad behavior of Abram in Genesis 12:10-20 with Romans 3:23 and Romans 4:8.

2 a. Who suffered because Abram sinned?

126

b. Do you believe that when a person sins today others are hurt by his disobedience to God? Think of some situations where sin not only hurts the person who sins, but also the person's family, friends, and associates. Share your thoughts with your discussion group, if possible.

c. What wonderful promise does God make to you in 1 John 1:9?

d. (Personal) Examine your own life actions and your innermost thoughts and emotions. Is there anything that you need to ask the Lord Jesus' forgiveness for right now? Stop now and ask Him. Then thank Him for forgiveness!

3 a. What part of Canaan did Abram return to and who was still with him? See Genesis 13:1.

b. What place did Abram revisit and what did he do here?

c. Do you believe that Abram confessed his sin to God at this time and asked His forgiveness? What phrase in Genesis 13:4 would suggest this?

4. What brought trouble between Abram and Lot's herdsmen? Give verses.

5 a. How did God lead Abram to solve the problem and settle the quarrel?

b. (Personal) Abram was older and could have demanded his right by age to have the best land, but he didn't! Have you ever chosen to give up your "rights" to bring peace into a difficult situation? If possible, share with your discussion group.

c. Relate how you could use this story to teach a child how to give up his rights to keep peace with a friend or brother or sister.

d. Surely God was helping Abram to make this unselfish decision. How could Zechariah 4:6 be applied to this situation?

6 a. Where did Abram go to live and what was the first thing recorded for us that he did there?

b. (Personal) Do you meet with God the first thing in the morning, at least for a few minutes before you start your day? As a family, do you meet with God around the breakfast table for a few minutes? God is eagerly waiting for you to want to do this. Will you trust Him now to help you to do this? See Philippians 4:13.

c. Which verse did you choose to hide in your heart this week?

BELIEVING THE PLANS AND PROMISES OF GOD
GENESIS 10-13

Study Notes

Among stories of the world's history, the story of the Flood is the most common. From China to the pre-Colombian Indians, and among the American Indians, we find many forms of the flood story which have passed from generation to generation. Many of these stories have rather unusual or odd descriptions of the boat and other details of the Flood because of the failure of man's memory. *Yet men everywhere have a record of the Flood, and in the Bible we find the history of the Flood preserved by God for us.*

Many other passages in the Bible confirm the history of the Flood. For instance, Isaiah 54:9 records, "For this is as the waters of Noah unto me: for as I have sworn that the waters of Noah should no more go over the earth; so have I sworn that I would not be wroth with thee, nor rebuke thee." Thus God is saying that His promise is as sure as the events concerning the historic fact of the Flood.

In 2 Peter 2:5 we read, "[God] spared not the old world, but saved Noah the eighth person, a preacher of righteousness, bringing in the flood upon the world of the ungodly." We notice here another historical detail. Noah was a preacher of righteousness and was the eighth person, along with seven others of his family, who was saved in the ark.

129

The Record of Noah's Sons Genesis 10

Genesis 10 contains a record of the generations of the sons of Noah; Shem, Ham and Japheth. Abram was a descendant of Shem (Genesis 11:10-27). Abram now becomes the main figure of Genesis. Physically he was the father of the Hebrew nation (Genesis 12:2,7; Genesis 13:15,16).

He is also the ancestor of Christ, as Joseph directly descended from Abram (Luke 3:23-38). Abram was also a pioneer of faith in God's promises (Hebrews 11:6,8-12). All who are born again through faith in Jesus Christ are called the spiritual children of Abraham in Galatians 3:29.

Abraham was called "righteous" because he believed God's Word and obeyed. We are also counted righteous when we believe God's Word concerning salvation by faith in Jesus Christ. "Of this man's seed hath God according to his promise raised unto Israel a Savior, Jesus" (Acts 13:23). This verse was speaking of David who was the descendant or seed of Abraham.

God makes it clear in Genesis 10 that the three sons of Noah became the fathers of the three great families of mankind. Genesis 10:2-5 tells us of Japheth who became the father of one large branch of the Gentile world. Genesis 10:6-20 tells us of the descendants of Ham who became another branch of Gentiles including Egyptians, Ethiopians, Libyans, and kindred groups. His son, Canaan (Genesis 10:15), became the father of the Canaanites, the inhabitants of the land of Canaan, who were later dispossessed by the Hebrews. The curse pronounced by Noah in Genesis 9 on Ham's descendants was not in any sense designed as a proof text for slavery or segregation.

In Genesis 10:21-32 we learn that Shem's descendants were called the children of Eber (Genesis 10:21) which is the name that the word "Hebrew" comes from. *Shem's descendants would become the spiritual leaders of men, whom God would use to teach the religion of Jehovah to the world.* The Lord Jesus Christ, the Messiah, was to come from Shem's descendants.

Just as Shem's descendants had a responsibility to teach about Jehovah, the Christian today has a responsibility to share the Lord Jesus Christ with others. We are told to teach our children and grandchildren about what God has done for us through Jesus Christ. We are to share this great truth with others as the Holy Spirit leads us.

If you are a Christian, are you doing these things? Do you keep the Word of God in your heart and teach it to your children or to others of your acquaintance? *Are you using every opportunity that the Holy Spirit affords you—when you sit in your house, when you walk with a friend, when you are resting, or visiting, or when you are at work?*

(Deuteronomy 6:6,7; 1 Timothy 3:4,5; Deuteronomy 4:9,10; Proverbs 22:6.)

Man Fails God Genesis 11

The first children of Noah and their families traveled together. They journeyed from one place to another to find the best pasture for their flocks and the best land on which to raise their fruits and vegetables. In their travels they arrived at a very fertile plain in the land of Shinar, the land between the rivers Tigris and Euphrates (Genesis 11:1,2).

Shinar must have been a very wonderful place to live. Two large rivers provided the water, and the best soil from the surrounding mountains had washed down to the plain during the Flood. Plants must have grown rapidly since there were no rocks in the soil.

The people discovered that they could make brick from the soil (Genesis 11:3). They formed clay into bricks and burned them with fire to harden them. The "slime" used to mortar the bricks together was really like the tar we use today in building roads.

Men may seem to be making plans opposing what God would desire for the world, but our hearts need not fail us. He is vitally interested in us and, by His power and might, He will protect us.

Because they were so successful in making bricks and building with them, "the people who lived there began to talk about building a great city, with a temple-tower reaching to the skies—a proud, eternal monument to themselves. 'This will weld us together,' they said, 'and keep us from scattering all over the world.' So they made great piles of hard-burned brick, and collected bitumen to use as mortar" (Genesis 11:3,4).

Notice the number of times these people use the word "us" and "we" in just one verse! How many times do they mention God? God had told them to be fruitful, multiply and replenish the earth (Genesis 9:1,7). They were following their own selfish plans rather than obeying God. Can't you just hear them saying to each other, "People are going to remember us now. We are making a name for ourselves"? And they watched the walls of the tower rise higher and higher.

God has tested man under every conceivable condition and found him wanting. We find this true in the land of Shinar. In our day there are those who think that bettering man's environment will help them; they forget the beautiful environment of the Garden of Eden! Others think that education will save man, forgetting that the knowledge of good and evil was received at the time of the fall of Adam and Eve (Genesis 3:22). Still others believe that something like a United Nations can enforce righteousness and peace in the world.

Shinar proves to us that none of these methods will work! It shows us that man did not fall merely once in the Garden of Eden, but that man always falls when confronted with fresh conditions that reveal his true human desires. "For all have sinned, and come short of the glory of God" (Romans 3:23). Thus God realized that He had to provide a way of righteousness.

Romans 3:21-26 explains the way of righteousness which God has provided for you. "But now God has shown us a different way to heaven—not by 'being good enough' and trying to keep his laws, but by a new way (though not new, really, for the Scriptures told about it long ago). Now God says he will accept and acquit us—declare us 'not guilty'—if we trust Jesus Christ to take away our sins. And we all can be saved in the same way, by coming to Christ, no matter who we are or what we have been like" (Romans 3:21,22). Have you come to God by faith in the Lord Jesus Christ? Are you sharing your faith with others?

The sin in Shinar was the sin of self-sufficiency and pride in one's own work. These people said, "let us" rather than "thy will be done" (John 4:34; Luke 22:42). These people were saying, "Let me" instead of "Lord, do it all." Which of these phrases do you use in your prayers? When God lets man do what he wants to do, then there comes failure and frustration. If we ask God to "do it all" we discover that God's ways are "pleasantness, and all [His] paths are peace" (Proverbs 3:17).

Some people believe that these men were actually trying to build a tower that would reach to heaven. How foolish they were if that is what they were trying to do. The only way to reach heaven is by faith in the Lord Jesus Christ (John 14:6). Others think that they wanted to build a great high tower for a temple, on top of which was a zodiac by which the priest hoped to get knowledge from the stars. No matter what they were trying to do, they were very foolish to leave God out of their plans!

In Genesis 11:5 we find that the Lord came down to see the city. *The Lord is not only aware of all that goes on in this earth, but He is vitally interested in all that takes place.* Not a sparrow falls without His knowledge, and the very hairs of our heads are numbered (Matthew 10:29,30). "His eyes behold, his eyelids try, the children of men" (Psalm 11:4).

Today, God on His throne still watches men make plans, and He will not let evil conquer in the end (2 Chronicles 20:6; Psalm 1:6). As

132

Christians we need to remember, "If God be for us, who can be against us?" (Romans 8:31). Men may seem to be making plans opposing what God would desire for the world, but our hearts need not fail us. He is vitally interested in us and, by His power and might, He will protect us.

God realized that nothing on earth would be restrained from these men (Genesis 11:6), so He decided to restrain them by His power. He confounded their language (Genesis 11:7). The variety of tongues was not ideal: it was "babel."

The diversity of language is confusion. It is a judgment upon human defiance of God's law that men should scatter normally and repeople the earth He had made for their enjoyment (Genesis 9:1). *But God tempered His judgment with mercy. He did not disrupt families.*

Babylon and Egypt were founded by Ham (Genesis 10:16-20). The descendants of Ham found their home in Africa where they dwell to this very day. Shem settled in Persia and from Mesopotamia to Asia. Assyria was founded by Shem (Genesis 10:11,12,21-31). Japheth, founder of the European nations (Genesis 10:2-5), inherited both Europe and Asia.

Look back over the story as it is told in Genesis 11 again. What brought about this judgment of God? What exactly had the people done?

First, they were disobedient. The Lord had told Noah that he and his sons were to replenish the earth, not just a part of the earth, but all of it. The people disobeyed the command of God (Genesis 11:2). This is the same kind of sin that Adam and Eve committed. The people after the Flood were disobedient to the commands of God. *When you think about it carefully, you will see that sins begin with disobedience to God.*

Second, these people were proud. They were more interested in assuring fame for themselves than they were in obeying the Lord (Genesis 11:4). These people felt the necessity of being famous and making a name for themselves. They wanted others to be aware that they were around.

Is pride not often the cause of our sinning? Public opinion and public acclaim are strong influences upon most of us. We don't want to go against the crowd. We want people to like us and think well of us, and so we do things that we know are not the very best. *Let us beware of seeking to make a name for oneself even in Christian circles! Instead, we must choose deliberately to honor God's name and obey God's Word.*

Third, these people wanted to get to God in their own way (Genesis 11:4). They wanted to build a tower that would reach toward heaven. God is only pleased with those who worship Him in Spirit and

133

in truth. *If we love the Lord because He has saved us, we know there is nothing we can do with the works of our hands that will gain our access to heaven. We know we must come God's way (Matthew 7:14).*

In Genesis 11:30 we learn that Sarai, Abram's wife, was barren. She was to produce the seed by which God promised He would make a great nation (Genesis 12:2) and bless all the earth (Genesis 12:3). From Sarai and Abram's seed, the Messiah—the Lord Jesus Christ— would be born.

In Genesis 11:31, we learn that Abram's father, Terah, was with him on his journey to Canaan. Abram was from Ur of Chaldees (Genesis 11:28). No doubt, he had lived all his life in this city. Now the Lord was telling Abram that he should leave his home. Abram was obedient. There seemed only one wise way to travel, and that was north along the river Euphrates. The little group consisted of Abram, his wife Sarai, his father Terah, and his nephew Lot. They traveled along the river for 430 miles until they came to the city of Haran.

Abram disobeyed the Lord when he brought his family with him. God had said to leave his family and kindred (Genesis 12:1). It was wrong to stop at Haran. Terah probably created a great emotional scene at the old home in Ur when his son announced that God had called him to go to a far country which he had never seen. Finally, the old man said that he would go, too.

Since Terah had the authority of the father, Abram deferred to his wishes and there was the long wait at Haran. Thus, Abram lost several years by allowing his father a part in the action that came from the call and command of God. Terah was a devil worshiper and he managed the party on the journey according to his own earthly ideas, not according to the simplicity of God's command (Joshua 24:2).

They stayed in Haran for some time. Abram's father, Terah, actually died there at 205 years of age (Genesis 11:32). Abram then left this city which was noted for its idolatry and worship of the moon. Together with his nephew, Lot, and Sarai, his wife, he went into an unknown land at God's command.

Perhaps you have been walking away from God and have heard His call to walk into an unknown land through faith in His Son the Lord Jesus Christ. Are you willing to become the pioneer of your family as Abram was in his? Are you willing to blaze a new trail and walk with living faith in God?

God's Promise to Abram Genesis 12

Abram was to move to a place God would show him. Just think of what it must have meant for Abram to start out with his wife, nephew, and servants and move away from the river into the desert.

The next stop was Sichem which was over 300 miles away. Surely the only thing that kept Abram going was God's promise "I will show you a land" (Genesis 12:1).

The call of Abram was the beginning of a new development in the Messianic line. The line had run through individuals from Seth to Shem, covering a period of many centuries. Now it was to take a national form and Abram was selected as the head of that nation, the Hebrews. The chosen nation was born in faith, and was sustained by faith—the faith of its head, Abraham (Hebrews 11:6,8-12). The covenant is found in Genesis 12:1-3.

God promised to make Abram a great nation, make his name great, and bless him. Abram was determined to have that blessing from God so we read, "Abram departed, as the Lord had spoken unto him" (Genesis 12:4). *Abram was obedient to God and thus became a blessing to all generations as his descendants provided the human line through which Jesus Christ was born.*

Sin begins in the mind.... As we act upon it, sin progresses. We need to stop and ask God to forgive us and cleanse us at the moment a thought passes into our mind before it progresses into an act of sin. God is always willing to forgive us.

If we want to be a blessing as Christians, we must meet God's condition—obedience. Are you willing to meet this condition? Are you willing to take time daily in prayer and Bible study so that you can hear God and be obedient to what He asks you to do as you listen to Him? Why not stop right now and pray and ask God to show you your best time for prayer and Bible study. Ask Him, by the Holy Spirit, to give you the desire to take time each day with Him.

At last Abram arrived in the land he had been promised. Canaan or Palestine has been called the center of the earth. The borders were roughly from Dan to Beersheba and from the river Jordan to the sea. Here Abram and his children lived for many years and became great and powerful.

Abram was one of the great men of the Bible. *He was not great because he never made a mistake. He was great in the sight of God because he believed God.* "He staggered not at the promise of God through unbelief; but was strong in faith, giving glory to God; and being fully persuaded that, what he had promised, he was able also to perform. And therefore it was imputed to him for righteousness" (Romans 4:20-22).

135

In Genesis 12:7 we discover that one of the first things that Abram did when he reached Canaan was to worship God. Again, when he moved up the mountain on the east to Bethel, he pitched his tent and built an altar to the Lord and called upon the name of the Lord. God directed Abram in the many paths he took. The Lord brought him all the way from Ur to the Promised Land. Surely this must have been a time of great thanksgiving to God for His faithfulness in keeping His promises to Abram.

God keeps His promises to us today, also. Won't you begin to underline the promises which you find in the Bible and claim them for yourself today?

When a famine threatened his family Abram left the place of blessing and went to Egypt to live. *God often allows a testing like this to come to us to see if we will trust Him in spite of everything.* Sometimes we forget to trust God, just as Abraham forgot to trust God (Genesis 12:10). When we don't trust God, it only brings us trouble as it did for Abram. The only thing to do then is to confess our sin and go back and start again with God as Abram did (Genesis 13:4; 1 John 1:9).

Abram feared Egypt's Pharaoh and so, without asking counsel of the Lord, he took a step to avoid further trial. He had forgotten the promise of God concerning the seed which was to come from his marriage, and allowed his wife to go into the palace of Pharaoh. God, by divine intervention, protected Sarai so that she could be the mother of many (Genesis 13:16). God intervened by causing a plague on the house of Pharaoh (Genesis 12:17).

Abram suffered the shame and humiliation of a man who, having trusted God, was now sent away like a dog with his tail between his legs. Sarai was also hurt by Abram's disobedience in not trusting God, for certainly she must have been discouraged and frightened in her position in Pharaoh's house. Today when a person sins, others are hurt by his disobedience to God also.

Sin begins in the mind. Abram first thought of asking Sarai to tell everyone that she was his sister (Genesis 12:13). *Then Abram put his thoughts into words, and asked Sarai to tell others that she was his sister.* As we act upon it, sin progresses. We need to stop and ask God to forgive us and cleanse us at the moment a thought passes into our mind before it progresses into an act of sin. *God is always willing to forgive us as He forgave Abram.*

Abram Returns to His Land; Abram and Lot Separate Genesis 13:1-13

Trouble began to brew between Lot and Abram as their herdsmen quarreled over the land (Genesis 13:5-7). Abram and Lot's wealth lay in their flocks and herds (Genesis 13:2,5). Great riches had been given them in Egypt (Genesis 12:16) so there was no longer sufficient pasture for their herds in Canaan. *Abram revealed his trust in God once again by determining to avoid strife and by choosing faith in God to take care of him in regard to the choice of land. He allowed Lot to have the first choice (Genesis 13:9).* Abram undoubtedly knew that Lot would choose the best land and yet he strove "to keep the unity of [God's] Spirit in the bond of peace" (Ephesians 4:3).

Have you ever given to God something that cost you to give? Are you selfish about your time or are you willing to sacrifice the best of it so that you may share with others the Lord Jesus Christ? Have you ever given a love gift of money that is actually a sacrifice? Have you ever opened your home to a person in need, because you love God and desire to show your love by this sacrifice? Are you willing to suffer personal loss in order to end contention between yourself and another person?

These are steps in a practical walk of faith. And it is through such experiences that we learn that we can never outgive God. He always gives more satisfaction than we give to Him! Will you ask the Holy Spirit this week what sacrifice God is calling you to give to Him in love and obedience?

Lot was not upset by the strife. He revealed his selfishness by the choice he made. In Genesis 13:10 he chose the plain of Jordan that was well watered like a garden. Lot's main objective is similar to many today—to get the best of this world's goods. *Abram had said, "Let there be no strife" (Genesis 13:8), but one wonders if Lot would have fought to get the best of the land.*

What about in your home or in your relationships? Do people hear you raise your voice in anger wanting your own way? Or have you asked the Holy Spirit to help you to be the first one to give up your "rights" in an argument?

Lot chose to ignore and not admit that "the men of Sodom were wicked and sinners before the Lord exceedingly" (Genesis 13:13). He pitched his tent toward Sodom. Lot, his wife, his family, and servants would all suffer the results of such an evil environment. Lot did not choose a place which would bring his family close to God. He did not consider their surroundings.

Do you consider the influences of your society and community on your family's welfare and happiness? *We need to choose, if possible, everything concerning our families with a view of how it will bring them close to God by faith.*

Study Questions

Before you begin your study this week:
1. Pray and ask God to speak to you through His Holy Spirit each day.
2. Use only your Bible for your answers.
3. Write your answers and the verses you have used.
4. Challenge questions are for those who have the time and wish to do them.
5. Personal questions are to be shared with your study group only if you wish to share.
6. As you study look for a verse to memorize this week. Write it down, carry it with you, tack it to your bulletin board, tape it to the dashboard of your car. Make a real effort to learn the verse and its reference.

FIRST DAY: Read all of the notes and look up all of the Scriptures.

1. What was a helpful or new thought from the overview of Genesis chapters 10-13?

2. What personal application did you select to apply to your own life?

SECOND DAY: Read Genesis 13:8-18.

1. What did Abram say in Genesis 13:8 which should be the constant attitude in the life of the Christian?

2. We have many promises in the Scriptures concerning the help of the Lord Jesus Christ in all areas of our life including strife. Read the following promises and try to put them into your own words.

   2 Timothy 1:7

   Galatians 2:20

138

3. (Personal) Which of the promises in question 2 would you like to claim to help you this week in your problems?

4. Where did Lot pitch his tent and what kind of people was his family exposed to in this area? Give verses.

5. Lot made a poor choice for himself and his family by choosing to pitch his tent in the area of wickedness and sin against God. The Bible tells us the importance of choices in our lives. What does Joshua 24:15 say about making a choice?

6. **Challenge:** 1 Corinthians 3:9-15 describes a Christian and the testing of his service to God. How does this passage describe the Christian's eternal loss which he chooses if he makes a choice similar to Lot's choice?

THIRD DAY: Read Genesis 14, concentrating on Genesis 14:1-16.

Note: These verses describe five separate events happening over a fourteen year period of time:

1. Genesis 14:1-3—Kings from the East conquer kings of the area where Lot lives.
2. Genesis 14:4—The conquered people in Lot's area rebel.
3. Genesis 14:5-7—Eastern conquerors move southward toward the Dead Sea area, conquering the people along the way.
4. Genesis 14:8-12—The local kings battle with these eastern conquerors near the Dead Sea; Lot is captured.
5. Genesis 14:13-16—Abram heroically rescues Lot and his family.

1 a. According to Genesis 14:4, how many years did the kings mentioned in Genesis 14:1 serve their conquerors from the East?

b. What did these local kings do in the thirteenth year?

2 a. The Vale of Siddim (near the Dead Sea) where they fought was full of what?

b. What happened to two of the kings in the Vale of Siddim and who were they?

c. Where did the defeated local troops flee?

3. What did the conquering kings and their troops take after they won the battle at the Vale of Siddim?

4 a. An escaped soldier told Abram about Lot's capture. What action did Abram take to help Lot?

b. Was Lot rescued? What else was rescued?

5. God used Abram to rescue Lot in this battle. Who then strengthened Abram and enabled him to win this battle? See Psalm ·24:8 and Psalm 50:15 and relate God's help to your present "battle."

6. Just as Abram triumphed in the battle, we are promised victory through the Lord Jesus Christ. What do you find most helpful or challenging about the promise in 2 Corinthians 2:14,15?

FOURTH DAY: Read Genesis 14:17-24.

1 a. What two kings honored Abram after his victory in battle, and what did one king bring with him?

b. What do you learn about Jesus Christ and Melchizedek in Psalm 110? This is a Messianic Psalm speaking of the Lord Jesus. Give verse.

c. **Challenge:** Read Hebrews 7:1-3 and list all of the new facts you learn about Melchizedek in this passage.

d. **Challenge:** Read Hebrews 7:22,24-27 which describes Jesus Christ as our High Priest. List the blessings we have from Jesus Christ as our High Priest.

2. According to Hebrews 7:4 and Genesis 14:20, what did Abram give Melchizedek?

3 a. What does God promise in Malachi 3:10 to those who will give a tenth of their earnings to Him?

b. (Personal) Will you trust God to keep this promise in your life?

141

4. Was Abram willing to receive gifts from the King of Sodom? Give reason why.

5. Who was it who had delivered the enemy into Abram's hands and made him the victor in the battle? Give verse.

6 a. **Challenge:** If you are discouraged, tempted by sin, fearful of some situation, or feel in need of Jesus Christ's help in some other way, what does Hebrews 4:14-16 say that encourages your heart today?

   b. (Personal) Why not stop right now and "lift up your hand" to God in prayer as Abram did? Ask Jesus Christ, your High Priest, for help.

FIFTH DAY: Read Genesis 15, concentrating on verses 1-5.

1. What did God promise He would be to Abram, so that he should not fear the future?

2. The Lord always provides armor for His people in the warfare they are in. Read Ephesians 6:10-18.

   a. Why did God provide the believer with spiritual armor according to Ephesians 6:11?

   b. Do you have your helmet on? What does this spiritual headpiece represent? See Ephesians 6:17 for what the helmet represents. Who made this headpiece available? Read 2 Timothy

1:9 and 2 Timothy 2:10 and rephrase these verses in your own words.

c. What part of the armor is the sword of the Spirit? Give specific ways that you use it daily.

d. After we have put on our spiritual armor, what are we to do according to Ephesians 6:18? Are you doing this?

e. Name the other parts of God's armor which a believer has available. See Ephesians 6:10-18.

3. **Challenge:** As Christians we need not fear the power of Satan or the world against us. Put the following verses into your own words to express your confidence which God's armor provides when you receive Jesus Christ by faith.

Isaiah 54:17

Romans 8:31

4. The Lord always provides armor for His people and the armor is Himself. How does Colossians 3:3 (the last half of the verse) express this truth?

5. God had promised Abram seed (children) in Genesis 12:2,3. Had a child been born to Sarai yet? What did God tell Abram about the number of his offspring in Genesis 15:5?

6. Did Abram believe God? What was it counted for?

SIXTH DAY: Read Genesis 15:6-21.

1. Read Romans 4:17-22 about Abram's faith. Think of all of God's promises in the Bible to you. Read Romans 4:20 with this in mind and put this thought into your own words as you relate it to your life today.

2. What do Romans 4:22 and Genesis 15:6 say about Abram?

3. What does Isaiah 64:6 say about our own human righteousness (goodness)?

4. (Personal) Put Romans 6:11-13 into your own words. Have you been made alive to God by your faith in Jesus Christ? If so, will you now apply these verses to your own life today?

5. **Challenge:** What did God warn Abram that "his seed" would suffer? How would He rescue "his seed" from their difficult circumstances? See Genesis 15:13,14 with Exodus 1 and 14.

6 a. Again God promised Abram's seed the land in Genesis 15:18. According to this verse, what will the boundaries be? Find this on the map if possible.

   b. Which promise from God's Word did you choose to *believe* and *memorize* this week?

STEPS IN FAITH: PROMISE, PATIENCE, POSSESSION

GENESIS 13-15

Study Notes

Abram and Lot Separate Genesis 13:8-18

Abram pleaded in Genesis 13:8, "Lot, let there be no strife, I pray thee, between me and thee." Because there was not enough land to supply pasture for both Lot and Abram's flocks, Abram made the generous suggestion that Lot choose any section of the land he preferred and move in that direction.

Abram set an example here for every Christian by his words, "let there be no strife." We see selfish human nature expressed in Lot's immediate choice of the well-watered valley of the Jordan (Genesis 13:10). There was much tropical vegetation and the land was large enough and fertile enough to guarantee prosperity and plenty for Lot and his family. Lot's eyes were the binoculars of his heart.

Choices are made in the secret place of the heart long before they are actually acted out. Lot had a selfish nature, and these circumstances revealed his selfishness. The things which are seen are temporary (2 Corinthians 4:18). A man who sees only earthly springs does not realize how quickly the water level can fall. The man who learns that all of his springs are in the Lord (Psalm 87:7) needs never fear the desert.

The "best" land proved to be a disastrous choice. Lot moved himself and his family, step by step, into degeneration. *We can learn from his actions how a person can slip into a sinful atmosphere:*

1. He *looked toward* Sodom.
2. He *pitched* his tent *toward* Sodom.
3. He *dwelt in* Sodom. We need to ask ourselves if we have made a wrong choice and are moving step by step toward something that is contrary to God's plan for us as Lot did. Our prayer should be, "Teach me to do thy will, for thou art my God" (Psalm 143:10).

Abram dwelt in the land of Canaan (Genesis 13:12). God chose for Abram the land and invited him to open his eyes and feast upon the treasures that stretched out before him in every direction (Genesis 13:14). God also promised Abram many descendants, more numerous than the dust of the earth (Genesis 13:16). Who can count the grains of dust of this earth? Yet God said so shall the descendants of Abram be! In Genesis 13:17, Abram was instructed by God to walk through the land that He would give to him.

God promises us many things in the Scriptures. We are to possess the promises from Genesis to Revelation. *How many of God's promises are you claiming for yourself this week?* Are you going to "walk through" His promises to you by daily reading the Bible?

When Abram first came into the land, he dwelt in Bethel which means "house of God." He left that place for Egypt at the time of the famine. Now he went back, a more joyful and wiser man.

He now lived in Mamre (Genesis 13:18) which means "vision." He pitched his tent in Hebron, which comes from a verb meaning *join together.* At Bethel, Abram had worshiped; at Hebron, he knew true fellowship with God. Thus faith progresses to greater faith.

Again, as at Bethel, Abram built an altar to God at Hebron. He learned a great lesson in Egypt. We, too, can walk with God and acquire greater knowledge of and love for Him (Philippians 1:6).

The First War; Lot Captured Genesis 14:1-12

Abram spent most of his life in Hebron. It is a beautiful city approximately 3000 feet above sea level and 19 miles from the present-day Jerusalem. Hebron is surrounded by olive groves, grapes, springs and wells, and rich pasture. Abram bought a cave called Machpelah, near Hebron, for a tomb for his wife Sarai. Later Abram, Isaac, Rebekah, Jacob, and Leah were buried there.

Genesis 14 records the first war in the Bible. Wars come from the fallen state of man and from the lusts that war in the human race (Romans 3:23, James 4:1). The invaders were four kings (Genesis 14:1) and those attacked were five kings listed in Genesis 14:2. The

146

kings who were attacked were the kings of five cities that lay close together in the plain of Jordan (Sodom, Gomorrah, Admah, Zeboiim, and Zoar).

We read of the revolt of these subjugated people in Genesis 14:4. Growing weary of their conquerors, they rebelled by denying tribute money. The original battle was fought in the Vale of Siddim (Genesis 14:3). This area is largely covered by the Dead Sea today.

In the fourteenth year after the original battle, the four invading kings (Genesis 14:1) returned to Palestine to collect their tribute from the five kings of this area who are mentioned in Genesis 14:2. Genesis 14:5-7 gives us a blow-by-blow description of the battle. The five kings (Genesis 14:8) decided to make a last ditch stand in the Vale of Siddim. This area possessed a natural defense, great slime pits, in which they planned to trap their enemies. Yet the battle ended in complete defeat of the five kings by the invaders. The kings of Sodom and Gomorrah fled to the slime pits and hid there, while many of the fighting men fled to the mountains for safety (Genesis 14:10). The enemy plundered all of Sodom and Gomorrah and then began their trip northward, taking with them many captives including Lot and his goods (Genesis 14:12).

The Christian must wisely consider Lot's fate and distinguish himself from his non-Christian neighbors. This does not mean that we should totally disregard a non-Christian neighbor, for we are called to be witnesses for Jesus Christ in this world. However, we are not to live in the life-style of our non-Christian neighbors. Instead, we are to live guided by the Bible's truths and by the Holy Spirit's guidance and power.

When men abuse God's gifts of bountiful supply, God brings judgment upon them and strips them of what they have so abused. Lot shared with his neighbors in this common calamity. The Christian must wisely consider Lot's fate and distinguish himself from his non-Christian neighbors (2 Corinthians 6:16-18). This does not mean that we should totally disregard a non-Christian neighbor, for we are called to be witnesses for Jesus Christ in this world. However, we are not to live in the life-style of our non-Christian neighbors. Instead, we are to live guided by the Bible's truths and by the Holy Spirit's guidance and power (2 Peter 1:3).

Victorious Abram Rescues Lot
Genesis 14:13-16

In Genesis 14:13 one of the escaped warriors found Abram and told him of Lot's capture and the victory of the four foreign kings (Genesis 14:13). Abram helped Lot by rescuing him from his captors. *A man who is truly separated unto God has power to help others in time of need.*

Surrendered, praying Christians are important to our nation (James 5:16). Abram could have said, "It served him right," or "He had it coming to him." God gives His people sympathy and they know the inner meaning of "judge not, that ye be not judged" (Matthew 7:1). Abram restored Lot in a spirit of meekness. "Dear brothers, if a Christian is overcome by some sin, you who are godly should gently and humbly help him back onto the right path, remembering that next time it might be one of you who is in the wrong" (Galatians 6:1).

Abram immediately chose 318 trained warriors from his servants and pursued Lot's captors into Dan (Genesis 14:14). Abram was a great man who had many servants depending upon him and employed by him. Though he was a man of peace, he disciplined his servants for war. Our Christian faith teaches us to be for peace, yet it does not forbid us to go to war when there is just cause to defend someone. When the crisis came, Abram drew new strength from God and pursued victory.

In Genesis 14:16 we read that Abram brought back all of the goods, Lot and his goods, and the women and people. In Genesis 13 we saw a meek and lowly Abram yielding his rights to Lot. The present chapter shows us a courageous Abram, a man of decision and great ability.

How does a man discover his gifts? The answer is that his gifts are given by God. The Holy Spirit came upon some men to give them the gift of fine needle work (Exodus 28:39); to others He gave the gift of jewelry, masonry, woodworking (Exodus 31:3-5); to Joseph He gave the gift of good administration (Genesis 41:38). To Abram, God gave the gift of generalship—and with it the victory. Likewise God has given you gifts to meet certain needs.

An interesting note is that Abram rescued the rest of the captives for Lot's sake, though they were strangers to him and he was under no obligation to them. Abram could have brought back Lot alone by ransom, yet he recovered all of the women and the people and their goods (Genesis 14:16). *We can note from this that as we have opportunity we should do good to all people.* God does good to the just and the unjust and so must we (Matthew 5:45).

For the first time, Abram is called a Hebrew (Genesis 14:13). The word Hebrew comes from a root that means "passed over." Abram passed over the Euphrátes River; he was separated from Ur of the Chaldees, from his kindred and from his father's house even as the Lord had commanded him (Genesis 12:1). Other scholars believe that the word Hebrew means "a descendant of Eber."

Abram Meets Melchizedek, the Priest-king of Salem Genesis 14:17-24

Two kings came out to meet Abram after his great victory (Genesis 14:17-18): the king of Sodom and Melchizedek, king of Salem. The name of this mysterious king of Salem means either "king of righteousness" or "my king is righteousness." He was the priest-king of Salem, then the name of the present-day city of Jerusalem.

Melchizedek brought bread and wine for the refreshment of Abram and his soldiers and to congratulate their victory. As a priest of the Most High God, he blessed Abram which was undoubtedly a greater refreshment to Abram than were the bread and the wine. God raised up his Son, Jesus, several centuries later to bless us. "Unto you first God, having raised up his Son Jesus, sent him to bless you, in turning away every one of you from his iniquities" (Acts 3:26).

The second mention of Melchizedek is in Psalm 110:4, a psalm written specifically to prophesy the coming of the Messiah. Jesus referred to this psalm in speaking of Himself in Luke 20:41-44. In Psalm 110:4, the Messiah is said to be "a priest forever, after the order of Melchizedek." Hebrews 7:2 points out that Melchizedek is used as an illustration to portray the eternal work of Jesus as priest between man and God, as there is no record in the Scriptures of Melchizedek's birth or death.

We next meet Melchizedek in the book of Hebrews in Hebrews 5:4-6,10,11-14; Hebrews 6:20; 7:1-3,10,28. The main teaching of the book of *Hebrews* is that Melchizedek, in his relationship to Abram, points to the work of Jesus Christ as the High Priest for all Christians. Because of Jesus Christ's resurrection and ascension, Jesus is forevermore our priest (Hebrews 7:23-25).

Melchizedek offered bread and wine to Abram. In Matthew 26:26-28 and John 6:53-57, Christ gives to us spiritual bread (His flesh) (John 6:56) and spiritual wine (His blood) (Matthew 26:28) which strengthens the Christian for life and service for the Lord. *Do you think of this great blessing as you partake of communion in your church?*

Melchizedek blessed Abram in Genesis 14:19. He pointed toward Jesus Christ who blesses us in all spiritual blessings. "Blessed be the God and Father of our Lord Jesus Christ, who hath blessed us with all spiritual blessings in heavenly places in Christ" (Ephesians 1:3).

149

Melchizedek also received tithes from Abram (Genesis 14:20). Christ joyously receives tithes from us, from all the goods He has given us. Do you give Him at least one tenth of all He has given you every week? God promises in Malachi 3:10 to "open you the windows of heaven and pour you out a blessing, that there shall not be room enough to receive it" to those who give their tithes to Him.

Abram acknowledged his dependence upon the king of Salem by accepting his blessing and giving to him his tithe. He declared his independence of the king of Sodom by refusing to take any of the spoil of the battle which the king offered him (Genesis 14:21-23). Some people have had their heads turned by recognition from a king, but this was not so of Abram. When John Knox was asked if he were frightened by the prospect of meeting the queen of Scotland, he replied that he had just spent four hours with God! Such a man can't be impressed by a mere queen!

If we ask the Lord for something and do not receive it "by return mail" we feel that the Lord has said no. But this may not always be the case. The Lord often answers our prayers with "wait awhile." In His own good time, God gives us those things which He has promised and those things which are needed for our lives.

Abram was also close to God as revealed by his words in Genesis 14:22, "I have lift up mine hand unto the Lord, the most high God, the possessor of heaven and earth." *Because he was close to God, the great temptation which followed this great victory was conquered in God's strength.* Why should Abram want the spoil of a battle when he had God the possessor of heaven and earth!

Actually, the victor in a battle had the legal right to keep the spoils of war. Yet Abram refused to take even a thread or a shoe latchet for himself, although he did accept a portion of the offer for his allies (Aner, Eschol, Mamre—Genesis 14:24). Abram recognized that all his riches came from God. He knew that God had delivered the enemies into his hands (Genesis 14:20).

Frequently, when there is a great spiritual victory, a great temptation follows. We can learn from Abram how to conquer this temptation. He had experienced wonderful fellowship with the priest, Melchizedek, as we have fellowship with our High Priest, the Lord Jesus Christ. Abram had given the glory of the victory to God and we, too, should remember to give the glory of any victory to God.

Abram refused the rewards of the king of Sodom. Then God came to him and said in Genesis 15:1, "Abram, I am thy . . . exceeding great reward." God would give Abram the desire of his heart, what seemed impossible, a son from his own body.

God wants to be your "exceeding great reward" also. Do you recognize that your only true riches come from God?

God Declares His Promise to Abram
Genesis 15:1-6

This is the first time that the well-known phrase, "The Word of the Lord came to," is used in the Bible, and we note that it is used frequently from this time forth. The Word of the Lord came in many and varied ways (Hebrews 1:1). Christ said, "Sanctify them through thy truth: thy word is truth" (John 17:17).

The "Word from God" was given to Abram to meet his needs at this time. It wasn't easy for Abram to wait for God to give him a son. Waiting is never easy. When we want something, we want it now! We don't like to wait!

Abram was 75 years old when God promised that He would make of him a great nation. He had to wait 25 years until Isaac was born and the promise began to be fulfilled. No wonder this man is commended for his faith in the Lord's Word (Hebrews 11:8-10).

If we ask the Lord for something and do not receive it "by return mail" we feel that the Lord has said no. But this may not always be the case. *The Lord often answers our prayers with "wait awhile."* In His own good time, God gives us those things which He has promised and those things which are needed for our lives.

Abram's faith in God's Word earned him God's praise. *Remember, the Lord is pleased by faith in Him. Rest in His plan for you, knowing that He never makes mistakes.*

The four kings who were powerful enough to defeat the five kings were in turn beaten by Abram plus God! They certainly had the resources to regroup and come against Abram in another attack. It is at this point that God revealed to Abram that He is his ally, and therefore his shield (Genesis 15:1).

God in this same way tells us, "Don't be afraid, don't worry. I will protect you; I am your security and your shield." God's Word to Abram is a great comfort to believers who choose to risk their earthly security in some great cause for God and their fellow Christians.

The Lord Jesus Christ promised us, "My peace I give unto you . . . . Let not your heart be troubled, neither let it be afraid" (John 14:27). *Will you choose to reject fear and worry today because of God's*

151

faithfulness in being your shield? Have you taken up the shield of faith in the Lord Jesus Christ (Ephesians 6:16)?

It is good to remember that every time we serve the cause of Christ by spiritually helping another person, we may expect opposition just as Abram received opposition. When we choose to walk according to His plan for our life, we have God's secret unseen armor surrounding our lives. Have you thanked God today for being your shield?

God also reveals Himself as "thy exceeding great reward." No man has ever lost anything by giving up something for God. Abram had refused to take anything from the king of Sodom so that the king would not be able to boast that he had made Abram rich.

The Lord comes to those who put their trust in Him. "My God shall supply all your need according to his riches in glory by Christ Jesus" (Philippians 4:19). "Delight thyself also in the Lord; and he shall give thee the desires of thine heart" (Psalms 37:4).

Abram experienced God's provisions. He demonstrated his faith by addressing God, "Lord God," in Genesis 15:2. In Hebrew, this is *Adonai Jehovah. Adonai* means "master." Abram had learned to trust God and wanted to be His slave.

We see the human frailty in Abram as he goes on to say, "What wilt thou give me?" God had just told Abram not to fear and had promised to be his shield and reward. Yet ten years had elapsed since Abram arrived in the land, and the promise of his becoming a great nation was dim. He and his wife were beyond the age of child-bearing. To all outward appearances his heir was a servant who was born in his house and now was his steward (Genesis 15:3).

Abram conformed to the local custom current at that period and adopted a faithful servant he felt God would use to conceive the seed which He had promised. God assured him that the seed promised would come from his own body (Genesis 15:4). God did not name Sarai yet, which may account for Abram's confusion about how the seed would come, as recorded in Genesis chapter 16. God promised that Abram's descendants would be as numerous as the stars of the heavens (Genesis 15:5).

Not only Israelites after the flesh of Abram, but also believers in Christ are counted "the seed of Abraham." "And if ye be Christ's, then are ye Abraham's seed, and heirs according to the promise" (Galatians 3:29). In Genesis 15:7 God also promised that Abram's descendants would inherit the land of Canaan (Palestine).

In Genesis 15:6 we find the first mention of belief in God, "and he believed in the Lord." We know that there was faith in God before Abram, for God tells us of the faith of Abel, of Enoch and of Noah (Hebrews 11:4,5,7). By believing God's promise regarding an heir,

Abram proved his trust in God. He believed that one day God would send the Messiah. "And the scripture was fulfilled which saith, 'Abraham believed God, and it was imputed unto him for righteousness: and he was called the Friend of God'" (James 2:23).

Against all difficulties of age (Romans 4:19), Abram chose to believe fully that God would do for him what He had promised. God counted it to Abram for righteousness. Paul also wrote of this faith which was counted for righteousness in Romans 4:21-22. When Abram believed God's Word concerning the seed, Abram really believed in Christ (Romans 4:23-25). Have you been justified and accepted by God through your faith in the living Lord Jesus?

Before leaving this portion, we can learn something concerning our prayer life with God today. Abram's seed was promised to him before he entered Canaan in Genesis 12:7. Now ten years have passed, and because of Abram's age there was less and less chance of the promise ever being fulfilled. *Thus Abram poured out to God his discouragement and his deep question about this promise* (Genesis 15:2). The prospect was not encouraging and Abram spread his concern before the Lord.

God wants us to come to Him openly with our doubts, our desires, and our weaknesses. It is better to do this than to hide these things within our subconscious where they begin to fester and give us real problems. God recognizes our frailty and wants to help us. He is kind to us and is waiting to listen, so that He can work in our lives and encourage us through our fellowship in prayer with Him.

Do you have a heart-to-heart relationship with God? Do you share your deepest needs and doubts with Him? This is what God is longing for you to do.

In verse 4 we read, "And, behold, the word of the Lord came to him." It was a word of correction and one that revealed the tender heart of God. *God's tender heart is waiting to help you. Will you go to Him in prayer today and spread out before Him every need, both large and small?* Then you will be able to praise God as the psalmist did in Psalm 138:3: "When I pray, you answer me and encourage me by giving me the strength I need."

The Formal Transaction of the Covenant Promise Genesis 15:7-21

God promised Abram the land of Canaan and now Abram asked God for a confirmation of His promise (Genesis 15:8). The question, "Whereby shall I know that I shall inherit it?" came not from idle curiosity, but from a heart of faith. Abram was asking to be more clearly informed.

God answered Abram's request by requiring him to transact a formal contract, according to the ceremonial rites of that day. Since written agreements were rare, men made business transactions with solemn ceremony. The men involved were required to bring certain animals that were slaughtered, divided into pieces, and laid opposite each other in such a way as to leave a path in the center. The persons involved in the covenant or contract walked through this path. This represented the two men's agreement to the promise. Abram proved his faith in a practical way as he prepared the sacrificial animals for this covenant rite.

These verses may speak symbolically of several things. The sacrifices seem to represent Abram's seed (Genesis 15:9-10). The fowls seem to represent the enemies of Israel (Genesis 15:11). The burning lamp seems to indicate the glory of God in the midst of Abram's seed (Genesis 15:17).

God speaks of Abram's seed being "a stranger in a land that is not their's" (Genesis 15:13). He tells Abram that his seed will serve the people of this land and be afflicted for 400 years. We read in Exodus that Israel later was in slavery, in Egypt, for 430 years.

In Genesis 15:14 God revealed to Abram that God will judge the nation that held his seed in bondage. The judgment of Egypt, for their unjust treatment of Israel, is described in Exodus 6:6. In Genesis 15:15 God prophesied that Abram will be buried at a good old age and in peace.

In Genesis 15:16 we find that four generations will pass before Abram's seed will take possession of Canaan. Why did Abram's descendants have to wait four generations? We see the answer in the last half of Genesis 15:16, "for the iniquity of the Amorites is not yet full."

To possess the land, Abram's descendants would have to dispossess the Amorites (Canaanites) because of their exceedingly sinful influence. God was willing to wait approximately 400 long years before He gave His command for punishment and destruction of the people who lived in Canaan. He wanted to be sure that they had all refused to repent before He judged them. God did judge these Amorites for their sin eventually (Joshua 5:1, Joshua 12:1-2).

In Genesis 15:17 we see that the burning lamp passed between the divided sacrifices but Abram did not. This is God's personal assumption of all of the responsibility for His promise. What He promised, He will do! "In the same day the Lord made a covenant with Abram, saying, Unto thy seed have I given this land, from the river of Egypt unto the great river, Euphrates" (Genesis 15:18). As Abram responded by faith to God in this covenant, so we come in faith to the Lord Jesus Christ. Have you ever made a covenant with God as you

154

have heard His Word and believed on the Lord Jesus Christ? Read Ephesians 2:8,9 and put your name into three verses.

As God sent Abram to a new land, will you pray and ask Him what "new land" He will send you to this week? Is there a "new land" in your neighborhood, in your home, in your church, or in your community where the Lord wants you to walk with Him this week?

Study Questions

Before you begin your study this week:

1. Pray and ask God to speak to you through His Holy Spirit each day.
2. Use only your Bible for your answers.
3. Write your answers and the verses you have used.
4. Challenge questions are for those who have the time and wish to do them.
5. Personal questions are to be shared with your study group only if you wish to share.
6. As you study look for a verse to memorize this week. Write it down, carry it with you, tack it to your bulletin board, tape it to the dashboard of your car. Make a real effort to learn the verse and its reference.

FIRST DAY: Read all of the notes and look up all of the Scriptures.

1. What was a helpful or new thought from the overview of Genesis chapters 13-15?

2. What personal application did you select to apply to your own life?

SECOND DAY: Read all of Genesis 16, concentrating on verses 1-6.

1 a. According to the custom of her era, what Sarai suggested was legal and accepted as common practice by the people of that day. What was her suggestion in Genesis 16:1,2?

   b. Did Abram listen to Sarai's suggestion?

2. What were the sad results of Abram and Sarai's loss of patience and their desire to "help God" and hurry along the promised child (seed)?

3. Can you think of any ways that you or someone you know has tried to "help God" fulfill His promises, rather than completely trusting God to work out His promise and His plan in *His way* and *His time?* What were the results of these attempts?

●

4. **Challenge:** In many places in the Old Testament we are told to "trust" the Lord, be patient, and wait for His leading and help. Put the following verses into your own words as you relate their thoughts to your life concerning "trusting" and "waiting" on the Lord, rather than making your own human choices.

Deuteronomy 31:8

Psalm 37:5,7, and 40

●

Proverbs 3:5,6,24 and 26

5. What did the Lord Jesus Christ say about "trust" in Matthew 6:25-34? Summarize in your own words.

6. (Personal) Which of the thoughts from the Scriptures in question 4 or 5 would you like to appropriate in your life this week? Why? Share with your discussion group, if possible, to encourage others to trust God too.

THIRD DAY: Read Genesis 16:7-16.

●

1. After Sarai had dealt harshly with Hagar, where did Hagar go and who came to her there?

157

2 a. Had Hagar had anything to do with her present unhappy state? See Genesis 16:4.

b. What did Hagar lose by running away from a difficult situation? Use your imagination, as the Scripture is not specific on this!

3. (Personal) Ask yourself two questions concerning any problem you have today. What have I done to cause this problem to be more difficult then it need be? Am I trying to run away from the situation like Hagar, and in doing so, *what am I losing* by running away from my troubles?

4 a. What could a person do if he is part of the cause of his own difficulty? What would be better than running away from the problem? Read the following Scriptures to help you with your answer.

Colossians 3:13,14

Matthew 5:23,24

b. How could these verses help a person who has a difficulty with someone this week?

5 a. What was Hagar told to do by the angel of the Lord? Give verses from Genesis 16:7-14.

b. What did the angel of the Lord tell her about her son?

6 a. Who was the angel of God according to Hagar's words in Genesis 16:13?

b. What did she say to the angel of God?

c. Hagar returned to Abram's household as the angel of the Lord told her to do. How old was Abram when Ishmael was born?

FOURTH DAY: Read Genesis 17, concentrating on verses 1-14.

1. When Abram was 99 years old the Lord appeared to him. What did He tell Abram to do?

2 a. Since no person is sinless, God was asking Abram to be sincerely devoted and mature in faith toward Him in Genesis 17:1. What does Romans 3:23 say concerning any human being?

b. According to the following verses, who can make us and present us as "perfect" to God?

Colossians 1:27,28

Philippians 2:13

Revelation 1:5

3 a. In Genesis 17 what action did Abram take to humble himself before God?

b. (Personal) Do you ever take a "humble" position before God as you pray?

c. What does God again promise Abram in Genesis 17, which He has already promised in Genesis 12, 13, and 15?

d. What is Abram's new name given by God?

e. How long is God's covenant promise to last and how long are Abraham's descendants to have the land of Canaan for a possession?

4. What was to be the "outward sign" of the covenant promise which God had made to Abraham?

5. **Challenge:** The failure to be circumcised separated the general Philistine population from the children of Israel (Genesis 17:14). Not only was it a hygienic rite, but it also symbolized that the children of Israel were cutting off the sins of the flesh which their ungodly neighbors practiced. It symbolized their sincere devotion and mature faith in God. When Jesus Christ came, the rite of physical circumcision was abolished as a "sign of the covenant." What does Colossians 2:8-13 say concerning the "circumcision of Christ"?

6. (Personal) Have you ever invited Jesus Christ into your life so that He can present you as "perfect" to God through His forgiveness of your sins? How are you helping others to know your wonderful Savior?

FIFTH DAY: Read Genesis 17:15-21.

1 a. What new name did God give Sarai?

b. What blessings did God promise Sarah?

2. **Challenge:** What was Abraham's reaction to God's words? Do you think his reaction was joy, disbelief, or astonishment? Give a reason for your answer.

3 a. How did God answer Abraham's words which seemed to express his "human plan"—"Oh that Ishmael might live in thy sight"?

b. When you pray, do you ever offer a human plan of action to God as Abraham did in Genesis 17:18? What do you believe that God wants you to pray instead? (See the Lord Jesus' words in Luke 22:42 to help you think this through.)

4. (Personal) Can you think of any ways in which you are trying to tell God what to do and how to do it in your life? What comfort does 1 John 1:9 give you in this?

5. **Challenge:** What lessons do you learn about God's character in Genesis 17 as He responds to Sarah and Abraham's mixture of disbelief and faith in His promise of a son to them?

6 a. What does God say concerning His promise of a son to Abraham in Genesis 17:21?

161

b. (Personal) Have you trusted God for some promise from the Bible? Are you waiting for Him to work it out in your life? Are you willing to wait in faith for eleven or more years, knowing that He will keep His promises from His Word to you—just as faithfully as He kept His promise to Abraham? Share your thoughts with your discussion group on this question if possible. Share any experience of a promise God has kept in your life to encourage others.

SIXTH DAY: Read Genesis 17:22-27.

1. After God finished talking, what did Abraham do to show his faith and obedience to God?

2. (Personal) What action is the Lord leading you to take this week to show your faith and obedience to Him? Does He want you to "cut off" some activity so that you can spend more time in fellowship with Him through prayer and Bible study? Is there something else "of the flesh" that the Holy Spirit has been speaking to you about? Share, if possible, with your group.

3. What does Deuteronomy 30:6 say about circumcision inwardly?

4. What does Romans 2:29 say about circumcision?

5. **Challenge:** Put Romans 10:9,10 into your own words as you consider carefully your own "heart." Has your heart been spiritually circumcised by your faith in Christ?

6 a. (Personal) Are you teaching your household the truths of the

162

Scripture and leading them in the worship of God? Share with the group how God has led you in doing this.

b. Which verse did you choose to memorize this week?

GOD'S WILL IN GOD'S WAY IN GOD'S TIME

GENESIS 16-17

Study Notes

Sarai Gives Hagar, Her Maid, to Abram Genesis 16:1-6

In Genesis 15:6, we read of Abram's trust in God's promise: "He believed in the Lord; and he counted it to him [Abram] for righteousness." Now in Genesis 16, we see Abram's faith waver. Through unbelief he fathered a child who had no part in God's plan of inheritance for Abram's seed.

The birth of Ishmael marked the beginning of continuing strife over the land of Palestine, for Ishmael's heirs were to become a perpetual source of suffering and conflict for Abram's heirs—even to the present. Forming the nucleus of Palestinian Arabs even now, the descandants of Ishmael today still challenge the Jews—the descendants of Isaac—for the right to the land of Palestine.

In the time of Abram—and in many parts of the world today—barrenness was held in great reproach and often considered a punishment from God. To avert such a tragedy within a family, Eastern custom of that era required a childless wife to furnish a substitute "mother" to bear children for her husband. Usually a slave in the household was chosen to produce children for the wife who was unable to bear them. The wife was then able to regard any such children born of this arrangement as her own. And the children themselves became part of the household, receiving the protection and care of the man of the house.

Genesis 16:1,2 shows Sarai yielding to the pressure of the customs of the world by suggesting to Abram that he take her handmaid, Hagar, to bear him children. Sarai's suggestion would be unthinkable in our day, yet such a practice was acceptable procedure in that society. Scripture does not record, however, that Abram and Sarai ever went to God to ask Him whether their plan was His way of fulfilling His promise to them.

Can you think of ways that you have tried to "help" God fulfill promises to you from His Word, rather than completely trusting Him to work out His plan in His way and in His time? Do you attempt to use the customs of the world today to "help" God accomplish His plan for you?

Ten or more years had already passed since God had originally promised Abram a seed, so he acted upon Sarai's suggestion. Abram's acceptance of her plan was a mixture of faith and human reason, as Abram undoubtedly felt he could "help" God accomplish His plan with this poor human design. Culture excused Abram since local custom permitted his fathering a child by Hagar. But his action was not justified before God because the original biblical idea is one man, one woman (Genesis 2:24).

While Abram and Sarai believed the promise, the means by which they sought its fulfillment revealed a confused kind of faith that did not believe God would do the impossible. *If only Abram and Sarai had come to God in faith with their plan. If they had sought His will concerning the method by which He would fulfill His promise of a seed,* then think of the suffering Abram and his heirs would have avoided.

Can you think of ways that you have tried to "help" God fulfill promises to you from His Word, rather than completely trusting Him to work out His plan in *His way* and in *His time?* Do you attempt to use the customs of the world today to "help" God accomplish His plan for you? When we come to Jesus Christ in faith "old things are passed away; behold, all things are become new" (2 Corinthians 5:17).

DISCERNMENT
Lord, forgive me
 I opened my big mouth
  when I shouldn't have
   though I was really going to help you.

Well, I really made a mess of things,
   didn't I?
      Why?
I really thought you wanted me to say
   what
      I did.
Some things are better kept within the heart
   hidden from view
   shared only with you.
When am I going to learn that lesson, Lord?
   Discernment
      When to speak
         When not to speak?
Teach me by your Holy Spirit, Lord
Teach me discernment.

                                    By Doris Greig

"But this precious treasure—this light and power that now shine within us—is held in a perishable container, that is, in our weak bodies. Everyone can see that the glorious power within must be from God and is not our own" (2 Corinthians 4:7).

"I acknowledge my sin unto thee, and mine iniquity have I not hid. I said, I will confess my transgressions unto the Lord; and thou forgavest the iniquity of my sin" (Psalm 32:5).

"Yes I am the Vine [Jesus Christ]; you are the branches. Whoever lives in me and I in him shall produce a large crop of fruit. For apart from me you can't do a thing" (John 15:5).

As we abide in Christ, the miracle of His working out His plan through our lives will be fruit of eternal value. Our actions, our words, our thoughts, and our witness to others of the Lord Jesus Christ will please God as we abide in Him. Proverbs 3:4-6 gives the Christian some good advice. *"If you want favor with both God and man, a reputation for good judgment and common sense, then trust the Lord completely; don't ever trust yourself. In everything you do, put God first, and he will direct you and crown your efforts with success."*

Sarai and Abram's unwise decision had many repercussions. Sarai suffered by being despised by Hagar after the child was conceived (Genesis 16:4). Sarai and Abram also suffered, as their home was in turmoil, and Sarai blamed Abram for the situation. "My wrong be upon thee," meaning "It's all your fault" (Genesis 16:5). .

This story is an illustration of what happens when we take matters into our own hands and sin against God. We can only blame ourselves for the guilt and grief that follow us when we go outside of Gods plan and purpose for our lives. We can expect the same kind of turmoil in our lives as Abram and Sarai experienced during this period. We can also expect that others will be hurt by our actions just as the Egyptian maid Hagar was hurt by the actions of Sarai and Abram.

The Holy Spirit led Paul to write of this event in Abram's life as an allegory of the Christian life (Galatians 4:22-31). In this passage Ishmael is described as "born of the flesh" and is an illustration of man trying to fulfill God's purpose by his own efforts. The true life of faith is trusting in the Lord Jesus Christ and walking as the Spirit of God leads us by the inward power of the Holy Spirit (Romans 5:5; 1 Corinthians 2:10; 1 Corinthians 3:16).

Sometimes we don't stop to sit down when we are running away from unpleasant circumstances until we are too weary and thirsty to go on. But then when we do sit down in our "wilderness of trouble" and ask the Lord in prayer for His help and guidance, He gladly gives it to us. The Scriptures also guide us when we are in these "desert places" and the Holy Spirit speaks to us. God will meet you in your "wilderness" just as He met Hagar.

Look into your life. Do you see any confusion of faith and actions as illustrated by Abram and Sarai? Will you choose today to ask God to forgive you and cleanse you of any unbelief? (1 John 1:9). Now choose for yourself to seek God's plan and power for your life through the Holy Spirit.

God's Care and Promise to Hagar
Genesis 16:7-16

In Genesis 16:7 we find the first mention in Scripture of an angel's appearance. One wonders if Hagar might have been trying to get back to Egypt (Genesis 16:3), her homeland, for she was on her way to Shur which leads to Egypt. At any rate, she stopped at a spring to ease her weariness and have a cool drink of water. When the angel of the Lord asked her where she had come from and where she was going, she immediately answered truthfully (Genesis 16:8). We also see her obedience as she returns to the place where she has been treated harshly (Genesis 16:6), rather than trying to go on to her family in Egypt.

168

Sometimes we don't stop to sit down when we are running away from unpleasant circumstances until we are too weary and thirsty to go on. But then when we do sit down in our "wilderness of trouble" and ask the Lord in prayer for His help and guidance, He gladly gives it to us. The Scriptures also guide us when we are in these "desert places" and the Holy Spirit speaks to us.

God will meet you in your "wilderness" just as He met Hagar. Are you willing to sit down and spend some time with Him today? He will guide you with your problems just as He told Hagar what she should do. Will you wait on God?

"Commit everything you do to the Lord. Trust him to help you do it and he will" (Psalm 37:5).

"Rest in the Lord; wait patiently for him to act. Don't be envious of evil men who prosper" (Psalm 37:7).

"The steps of good men are directed by the Lord. He delights in each step they take. If they fall it isn't fatal, for the Lord holds them with his hand" (Psalm 37:23,24).

The angel went on to encourage Hagar by telling her of the mercy God had planned for her and the child she would bear (Genesis 16:11). Hagar was amazed that God saw and cared about her as an individual! (Genesis 16:13). She considered herself only an Egyptian maid who had run away from her unpleasant circumstances (Genesis 16:6), yet here we see God's tender ministry and guidance to her as an individual! What a joy she must have experienced to know that God cared about her welfare!

Do you sometimes feel mistreated, misunderstood, or even persecuted? Will you remember that God loves you as an individual? Sit down in a quiet place and let Him speak to you and guide you as you read the Bible and pray. Then obey God as Hagar did! She went back to Abram's family and bore her son (Genesis 16:15).

God Ratifies His Promise to Abraham and Sarah Genesis 17:1-21

The ratification of God's promise was the change of Abram's name to Abraham and Sarai's name to Sarah (Genesis 17:5,15). God made the change by adding the same sound (in Hebrew) to both their names. This change indicated that both were to be blessed with great posterity, for Abraham was to be "a father of many nations" (Genesis 17:4,5), and Sarah would become "a mother of nations" (Genesis 17:16). They would number even kings among their descendants (Genesis 17:6,16).

Before God changed it, Sarai's name meant "my princess," as if her honor were confined to one family only. Sarah signifies "a princess," namely "of multitudes," for her descendants would be so many. And now that she would have a son, she knew that the promise of Genesis 3:15 was hers and that from her descendants would come the Messiah.

Abraham's seed today is found "in many nations," for Scripture tells us that he is the spiritual father of those in every nation who come to God by faith in Jesus Christ:

"So God's blessings are given to us by faith, as a free gift; we are certain to get them whether or not we follow Jewish customs if we have faith like Abraham's, for Abraham is the father of us all when it comes to these matters of faith. That is what the Scriptures mean when they say that God made Abraham the father of many nations. God will accept all people in every nation who trust God as Abraham did. And this promise is from God himself, who makes the dead live again and speaks of future events with as much certainty as though they were already past" (Romans 4:16,17)

In Genesis 17:17 Abraham laughed in amazement and wonder that a child could be born to a man who was 100 years old and his wife who was 90! Is it possible that there could have been great joy in his laughter? Could it have been the laughter of delight rather than distrust? Only the Lord knows what was really in his heart, although it seems that Abraham believed what seemed too good to be true!

Is Abraham asking God to accept Ishmael in Genesis 17:18, "O that Ishmael might live before Thee!" or is he simply desiring that Ishmael not be abandoned by God? *The greatest thing we can desire of God for our children is that they may live and walk before Him in faith.* Perhaps this was Abraham's plea at this point for Ishmael.

Other Bible scholars feel that he was still trying to plan humanly how God would give him a son by presenting Ishmael to God. God promised to bless Ishmael in Genesis 17:20, "I have blessed him, and will make him fruitful, and will multiply him exceedingly." He tells Abraham that Ishmael will become a great nation.

Then in Genesis 17:21, God confirmed His promise of a son born of Sarah by confirming the time—"this season next year"—for the child's birth.

Abraham's Obedience as He Performs the Rite of Circumcision Genesis 17:22-27

Abraham carried out God's instructions to him concerning the circumcision of every male child over eight days old and of every male in his household whether that male was born in his house or bought with money from a foreigner (Genesis 17:11-13). Abraham's obedience to

God was immediate—"That very same day Abraham was circumcised, and his son Ishmael" (Genesis 17:26).

As God speaks to you through His Word, through prayer and fellowship, do you—in your situation—act immediately, obediently to the Holy Spirit's leading, as Abraham did? This pattern of immediate obedience is a good one for Christians to follow.

While the command is yet sounding in our ears, and a sense of duty is fresh, let us apply ourselves to it immediately. Then we will not deceive ourselves by putting it off for a more convenient time.

Abraham did not say, "I'll do this thing you ask me to do tomorrow, God." Because of his immediate obedience, he was ready to experience God's miracle of the birth of a son in his and Sarah's old age.

Are you willing to act in immediate and complete obedience to God, so you can experience His miracle in your situation?

The choice is up to you!

PRIORITIES

"I will instruct thee and teach thee in the way which thou shalt go: I will guide thee with mine eyes" (Psalm 32:8).

Lord, show me your priorities
for me
today
tomorrow
and always.

What were your priorities when you walked this earth?
To glorify God
and to be obedient to your Father's will.

What were Paul's priorities, Lord?
"According to my earnest expectation and my hope, that in nothing I
shall be ashamed but that with all boldness, as always, so now also
Christ shall be magnified in my body whether it be by life or death."

And what did James say, Lord?
"Our life is but a vapour that appeareth for a little time and then
vanisheth away. For that ye ought to say if the Lord will we shall live
and do this and that."

And what did you tell Peter, Lord,
he who denied you thrice?
What were his priorities to be?
"Feed my lambs, feed my sheep."

And Jesus said to Peter,
"I have prayed for thee that thy faith fail not and when thou art
converted strengthen thy brethren."

Please, Lord, show me your priorities for me.

Regal Books

Also Available in the Joy of Living Series. . . .

Courage to Conquer: Studies in Daniel—by Doris W. Greig
A Joy of Living Bible Study in Daniel. This is an in-depth look at a companion of kings, leader of men and a man truly devoted to his God. Today's world can learn from his uncompromising example. A 6-week study. 5419489

Walking in God's Way: Studies in Ruth and Esther—
by Ruth M. Bathauer and Doris W. Greig
A 7-week Joy of Living Bible Study. Learn about God's special love for us and how He is leading our every step. Explore how circumstances never stand in the way of God's perfect plan for our lives. 5419474

Power for Positive Living: Studies in Philippians and Colossians—
by Doris W. Greig
This Joy of Living Bible Study focuses on the Christian life of joy and hope as expressed in Philippians and Colossians. We can be joyful, even in a world of sorrow, and resist the powers of evil if we stand fast in the knowledge of our Lord. 5419493

Exercising a Balanced Faith: Studies in James—by Doris W. Greig
Granted that we are saved "by grace through faith"—what is the role of good works? This 8-lesson course explains James' insistence that works demonstrate whether or not we have saving faith. 5419649

Living in the Light: Studies in 1, 2 and 3 John—by Doris W. Greig
Recent scientific studies have shown the healthy effects of plenty of light. This 6-lesson study explores what it means spiritually to live an enlightened life—walking in the light of God's Word. 5419501

Also available late in 1989:
Discovering God's Promises: Studies in Genesis 17-33

Studies in The Gospel of John, chapters 1-10

Coming in 1990:
Discovering God's Protection: Studies in Genesis 34-50

Studies in the Gospel of John, chapters 11-21

Available at Your Christian Bookstore

THE
JOY OF LIVING
BIBLE STUDY
SERIES

Founded by Doris W. Greig, this series is an evangelical, nondenominational program for individual, church, home or group use. Using the Bible as its textbook, this program is designed to help people know Jesus Christ as Savior and Lord and to live for the glory of God. For more information about this series write:

JOY OF LIVING BIBLE STUDIES
Box 129, Dept. R, Glendale, CA 91209
Or call 818-244-2665